James Rev. Robertson

Narrative of a Secret Mission to the Danish Islands in 1808

James Rev. Robertson

Narrative of a Secret Mission to the Danish Islands in 1808

ISBN/EAN: 9783348016285

Printed in Europe, USA, Canada, Australia, Japan

Cover: Foto ©ninafisch / pixelio.de

More available books at **www.hansebooks.com**

NARRATIVE OF
A SECRET MISSION TO THE DANISH ISLANDS IN 1808.

BY THE REV. JAMES ROBERTSON.

EDITED FROM THE AUTHOR'S MS.

BY HIS NEPHEW,

ALEXANDER CLINTON FRASER.

LONDON:

LONGMAN, GREEN, LONGMAN, ROBERTS, AND GREEN.

1863.

INTRODUCTORY REMARKS OF THE EDITOR.

HE following Narrative, now firſt given to the world, relates to an important incident in the great wars of the French Revolution.

The Miſſion of which the accomplishment is here related, was undertaken by the Rev. J. Robertſon, at the ſpecial ſuggeſtion of the late Duke of Wellington, who, immediately before engaging in the Peninſular

ſular War had, with that foreſight which diſtinguiſhed him, turned his attention to the advantages which would be gained to the good cauſe by obtaining the ſervices of the *élite* of the Spaniſh army, as well as by the counſel of their experienced commander.

The ſucceſs of the undertaking and the ſubſequent advantages derived therefrom gave proof of the foreſight and ſagacity of the Duke; both as to reſults and the ſelection of the agent who was to undertake the arduous and moſt dangerous taſk of opening the communications with Romana.

Mr. Robertſon was informed, on his way through Hamburgh, that three or four perſons, ſent by our Government

Government with the ſame object, had been diſcovered almoſt immediately upon their landing on the Continent, and, of courſe, ſhot. This information, alluded to in his narrative, I had from his own lips.

In the Appendix will be found an extract from Napier's *Peninſular War.* The author ſeems to have been fully acquainted with the facts relating to the Miſſion, as well as to the beneficial reſults which followed its ſucceſs, and alſo with the name of the agent of the Government. The extract from Bourienne, alſo in Appendix, is of much intereſt, and, although giving a rather fanciful account of Romana's conduct while quartered in Hamburgh, and aſcribing to him views and plans which,

which, at the time, he could not poſſibly have entertained, at leaſt not in connection with the ſubject of the preſent narrative, yet bears teſtimony to the importance of the defection and eſcape of the Marquis, and to the profound impreſſion which it made in Europe. He bears very lightly on the cenſure on himſelf and Bernadotte implied in the order for increaſed vigilance, for it was ſtated at the time that Buonaparte was greatly irritated at the occurrence, and at the negligence of his agents.

It is right that ſome reaſons ſhould here be aſſigned for the delay which has taken place in making public this important document.

It would have been clearly improper

proper and impolitic to have published it during the continuance of the war; and the hiſtory of its retention from publication is ſummed up in the following ſtatement.

In the year 1813 Mr. Robertſon left Dublin, where he had been reſiding after his return or eſcape from the Continent in 1809, and ſhortly after went abroad to forward the views of our Government. On the entrance of the Allies into Paris he repaired thither and put himſelf in communication with the Duke of Wellington, who had, I underſtood (from letters received), employed him on ſeveral occaſions in important affairs. Leaving Paris in 1815 he went to Ratiſbon. In 1818 he viſited Scotland for a ſhort time, returning

turning to Ratiſbon where he died in 1820.

In the year 1825 I came to reſide in London, and in 1826 or 1827 waited on Sir Charles Flint of the Iriſh Office, an old friend of Mr. Robertſon, and through him opened a communication with the Duke of Wellington. After ſome time I learned that the Duke would be pleaſed to have the peruſal of the MS.; but it was not then in a ſtate to be preſented to him. Various cauſes aroſe to delay the preparation of a copy till the end of the year 1839, when I left one at Apſley Houſe. This MS. was miſlaid, and every effort to recover it was unſucceſsful.

Conſidering that the Narrative poſſeſſes

poſſeſſes great intereſt, and relates to the ſecret hiſtory of the times which it helps, in ſome degree, to elucidate, and that there cannot, at this time, be any objection to its publication, I now lay it before the public.

ALEX. C. FRASER.

3, Doddington Groye,
Kennington Park.

CONTENTS.

Chapter

Contents.

THE NARRATIVE.

Chapter I.

The Miſſion Propoſed, and Accepted.

THE Duke of Richmond, in his travels through Germany, towards the end of the laſt century, viſited the city of Ratiſbon, and during his ſojourn there honoured with his acquaintance the inmates of an abbey of Benedictines, natives of Scotland, and eſtabliſhed at Ratiſbon, principally, to ſuperintend the education of Scottiſh youths. The Abbot Arbuthnot and ſeveral members of the community were

Chap. I.

1807.

Chap. I. 1807.

were to be ſeen in the firſt circles of that imperial city, where their extenſive acquirements, and of ſome among their number it may be ſaid, their brilliant talents, gave them a conſpicuous poſition. Travellers from the United Kingdom, eſpecially, found pleaſure in the ſociety of men of letters, familiar, as theſe were, with the language and manners of Germany, but attached by the ties of nature and of principle to the country of their birth.

The Britiſh Envoy generally availed himſelf of their ſervices as interpreters at the Diet; and indeed, ſo highly did he appreciate their uſefulneſs, and ſo great was his confidence in their integrity, that he not unfrequently commiſſioned them to act in his ſtead.

One of the fraternity in particular (Mr. Horn), a man of diſtinguiſhed ability,

ability, had rendered ſuch ſignal ſervice to the Envoy, and had thereby become ſo obnoxious to Napoleon, that he was forced, in 1804, to quit Ratiſbon and ſeek a ſafer abode where the power of the French Emperor was not yet paramount.

Some years before this event, I, being a member of the community of which I have juſt ſpoken, had returned to my native country, and as it chanced that at the time of the Duke of Richmond's appointment to the Vice-Royalty of Ireland, in the year 1807, I was a reſident in that part of the kingdom, I was induced to addreſs his Grace on his nomination to that high office; and, while putting him in mind of his condeſcending viſits to the monaſtery at Ratiſbon, to expreſs the deſire I felt to be employed in any public ſervice, conſiſtent with my profeſſion, that might

Chap. I.

1807.

might conduce to the general good. The anſwer I received was couched in the moſt gracious terms; it intimated that the Duke would keep the ſubject in view and would embrace, with much pleaſure, any opportunity of obliging a member of the community from which he had received ſuch hoſpitable attentions.

That theſe were not mere court promiſes, made only to be broken, I obtained aſſurance in an interview to which I was ſhortly admitted by Sir Arthur Welleſley, who then filled the office of Chief Secretary to the Lord Lieutenant. To that interview, unimportant as it was in itſelf, my memory reverts with lively intereſt. The impreſſion is ſtill freſh which the ſimple, frank demeanour of the yet undeveloped hero made upon my mind in the courſe of a hurried converſation of not more than

Chap. I. 1807.

than ten minutes. I was poſſeſſed with a conſciouſneſs equally indefinable and irreſiſtible that I was in the preſence of a maſter-ſpirit gifted with a capacity to make "all time to come his own." From this my firſt reception I ſeemed to feel that the man with whom I was converſing was one who could conceive and execute the mightieſt deſigns. Was my augury vain?

The Chief Secretary was ſoon called to attend his duty in Parliament; but not long after his departure I received a communication from him requeſting my attendance in London, whither accordingly I repaired without loſs of time, though as yet unappriſed of the ſpecific purpoſe which the journey was to ſerve.

Sir Arthur thanked me for my ready compliance with his ſummons, and intimated that an opportunity would

would ſoon be afforded me of evincing both my loyalty and my courage. I replied that there was no danger I would not cheerfully encounter in the cauſe of my country, and again profeſſed myſelf ready for any undertaking that would not diſcredit my clerical profeſſion.

Theſe ſentiments elicited a hearty approval on his part, and ſo our interview cloſed.

I naturally expected that I ſhould quickly hear from Sir Arthur again, but in this I was diſappointed : days and weeks paſſed on without any notification that my ſeaſon of actual ſervice had arrived. I began at length to look on the iſſue of the affair as altogether uncertain, and being little inclined to importune the Government, I determined rather to ſeek ſome clerical engagement, and was at length induced to enter the

the family of a Catholic peer as travelling companion and chaplain.

On the laſt day of May, 1808, I accordingly entered upon my new duties; but ſcarcely was I ſeated when a letter was put into my hands from the Iriſh Office, deſiring my attendance at the houſe of Sir Arthur Welleſley, in Harley Street.

On receipt of this meſſage, ſo long and ſo anxiouſly waited for, and ſo little expected at the moment, I felt greatly embarraſſed. To quit my new patron ſuddenly would be difficult; it would be uncourteous in a high degree to do ſo without explaining the cauſe. Yet, could that explanation be given? Or, on the other hand, could I draw back from my firſt engagement with the Government? On reflection I reſolved firſt to wait on the Secretary, and then be guided by circumſtances.

Sir

Chap. I.

1808.

Sir Arthur broached the buſineſs with his uſual affability, which immediately ſets at eaſe thoſe who have the honour of treating with him. "You tell me, Mr. Robertſon," ſaid he, "that you are a man of courage." "Try me, Sir Arthur," I replied. "Well, that is what we mean to do. Will you aſſiſt in reſcuing the Spaniſh army, now detained by Bonaparte in the north of Germany? Will you carry propoſals from the Britiſh Government to the Marquis de la Romana, the commander of that army?"

"Will I?—with the utmoſt alacrity, Sir Arthur, and not without ſome confidence of ſucceſs. I ſpeak the language of the country as well as a native; and if I gain acceſs to the Spaniſh General, my words may perhaps all the more readily find credit with him on account of my clerical character. Moreover, I feel the

the deepeſt intereſt in the cauſe of his nation, becauſe I view it not only as the cauſe of an oppreſſed people but as the cauſe of religion. It is, in truth, the cauſe of my own country and of every people of Europe againſt the moſt unjuſt and ambitious of uſurpers. If I fall, it is a ſacrifice I make to my country. In the courſe of nature I have not many years to live—let me, before I die, have the honour of attempting, at leaſt, to render an important ſervice to my fellow men."

"Then you will meet me at the Foreign Office, when I ſhall introduce you to Mr. Canning."

Punctual to the appointed time, I was conducted by Sir Arthur Wellesley through a private door into the apartments of the Secretary of State.

Being little accuſtomed to diplomatic or courtly forms, I, no doubt, made

Chap. I.
1808.

made an uncouth appearance when uſhered into the preſence of the Miniſter. Sir Arthur could not refrain from ſmiling at my viſible embarraſſment, and Mr. Canning, by his manner, ſeemed to think me ill-fitted for ſuch a miſſion. I, however, ſhowed the grounds of my hopes, and manifeſted ſo eager a deſire to undertake the taſk, that it was finally entruſted to me.

The Miniſtry had been informed that the Daniſh Fort on the Elbe, called Glückſtadt, was garriſoned by the Spaniards. The worſt place in the world for one charged with an enterpriſe like mine to land at; for the Danes were ſtill ſo much exaſperated againſt England on account of the affair of Copenhagen that they ſpared no pains to diſcover and puniſh emiſſaries from our Government. The information proved, however, to be be erroneous; Romana's army was not ſtationed at Glückſtadt.

It was admitted that the Government were not preciſely informed of the views entertained by the Spaniſh General in regard to the late uſurpation of Bonaparte. Mr. Frere, indeed, had been perſonally acquainted with the Marquis, and gave a very high character of him. It was on account of his known abhorrence of the ambition and tyranny of the Corſican that he had been removed from Spain by the traitor Godoy, who, in giving him the command of the Spaniſh force ſent to co-operate with the French in the north of Europe, had at once deprived his native country of her ableſt general and her choiceſt troops. This had been done two years before the treacherous dethronement of the imbecile Charles and Ferdinand; and

Chap: I.
1808.

little now did the Machiavel of Corſica think that ſo maſterly a ſtroke of policy was about to be defeated by the agency of a humble monk.

Next came the meſſage to be delivered. Mr. Canning referred that particular to Mr. Hammond, whoſe inſtructions to me were to this effect:—You will inform the Marquis Romana that our tranſports ſhall be at his orders, to convey him and his troops to any place or country he chooſes. We aſk nothing in return: we do not require that they ſhould fight for us: we ſimply deſire to put it in their power to withdraw from their preſent ſituation: we offer to carry them free of coſt to South America, to Minorca, to Canada, to England, or to Spain, at their option. Tell him Mr. McKenzie waits at Heligoland to receive his determination: that if Spain is reſolved to reſiſt

resist the Usurper, we are ready to co-operate with her by every means in our power: that our cavalry were never better mounted, our artillery never better served, that our soldiers of every rank long for an opportunity to measure themselves with the French on land: that we consider Spain as the fairest field of action, and thereupon await the invitation of its oppressed inhabitants. Other instructions in conformity with these were given to Mr. McKenzie, who was to correspond from Heligoland with me on one side, and with the Government on the other; and if the Marquis should be disposed to send any of his officers to that island Mr. McKenzie was empowered to conclude a treaty with him in form.

There remained on my part a request to prefer. "Permit me to mention now," said I, addressing Sir Arthur,

thur, my firſt friend, "that, although pecuniary advantage is not my moving principle, I have certain ſacred duties to fulfil. An aged mother and two ſiſters have ſtrong claims on me: I live more for them than for myſelf. This is all I wiſh to ſay."

Sir Arthur, after a few words privately interchanged with Mr. Canning, immediately took up a pen and wrote, in the name of the King's Miniſters, an aſſurance of liberal remuneration to Mr. Robertſon in the event of his ſucceſs, and a further promiſe that, in caſe of a ſiniſter iſſue to his undertaking, his relatives ſhould be provided for at the expenſe of the Government. This document remained in the hands of a friend in London.

Chap.

Chapter II.

Paſſage to Heligoland. Perils in the Weſer. Arrival at Bremen.

VERY preliminary having been completely arranged, we left London on the King's birthday (the 4th of June), amidſt the ringing of bells and the firing of the park and tower guns: a happy omen! Having reached Harwich the ſame evening, I was entered by Mr. McKenzie at the Alien Office as a foreigner, whom he was inſtructed to convey out of the kingdom.

A favourable breeze brought us

in

Chap. II.
1808.

in forty-eight hours to Heligoland, where on landing we delivered a letter to the Conſul, who received us very kindly. This official letter contained an order for Mr. N. to lay an embargo on all ſhipping, till ſuch time as Mr. Robertſon ſhould be ſafely landed on the oppoſite coaſt, and tidings to that effect ſhould have been brought back to the iſland. Unluckily, the Conſul was not informed by Government of the object of my miſſion, nor was Mr. McKenzie authorized to conſult him. The embargo, too, was but ill-obſerved; for the news of our arrival at Heligoland was conveyed to the continent, and my landing was thereby rendered much more difficult. Without much loſs of time, however, a boat was ordered to bring me to a ſmall iſland, cloſe to the mainland. On my arrival there I found that

CHAP. II.

1808.

that the attention of the French had been called to that ſpot: they had thrice in one week viſited every bed in the iſland, a circumſtance which portended no good to any one landing on it. The inhabitants humanely intreated me not to proceed, and with much difficulty were prevailed on to grant me ſhelter for that night only.

Although I had laid claim to the quality of perſonal courage, it will not ſurpriſe any one who knows human nature, that, having hitherto been little converſant with danger in its more formidable aſpects, I ſhould ſhrink from the imminent peril which now threatened me at my next ſtep. To ſtay on the iſland, or to proceed without a guide or paſſport or recommendation, I found equally impracticable. I reſolved early next morning to return to Mr. McKenzie,

Chap. II.

1808.

McKenzie, and lay all my fears and difficulties before him. From that kind and brave friend I received all the ſympathy and all the encouragement I needed; he ſpoke of dangers he himſelf had encountered, and of the mental diſturbance he had often had to ſtruggle with in confronting them: but he repreſented to me at the ſame time how ſerious a diſappointment it would be to our Government, and how great a diſcredit to thoſe engaged in the undertaking, were I to return *re infectâ*; that others would be found to offer themſelves for the ſervice, that he himſelf, could he ſpeak the language, would not heſitate to charge himſelf with it. In ſhort, his counſel prevailed and I determined not to relinquiſh my object without further trial. Of the judgment and energy diſplayed by Mr. McKenzie on this occaſion

occasion it is impossible to speak too highly. I regret my inability to do justice to his deserts.

The Consul, Mr. N., seemed now to be more in earnest about the unknown affair. As the embargo still nominally continued, he sent for a contraband trader who had two vessels in the harbour ready to sail. "You are anxious to get away, are you not?" said Mr. N. to the smuggler. "Very anxious indeed," replied the other. "Should my absence be observed I shall, no doubt, be arrested on my return. Suffer me to sail, for Heaven's sake!" "On one condition," said the Consul. "Name it!" "That you take a friend of mine ashore." "Not for any consideration, sir," answered the smuggler. "It is impossible." "Very well; since you will not oblige me, do not expect me to oblige you. The embargo

Chap. II.
1808.

bargo continues a fortnight longer; and reſt aſſured I know you; your borrowed name does not conceal you. I know your owners alſo. You belong to the houſe of N. V., and your name is B—." The ſmuggler faltered. "Well then, ſince it muſt be ſo, I agree to take charge of your friend; but he muſt ſtrictly conform to my directions, or I will not be anſwerable for the conſequences." "He ſhall," ſaid the Conſul. "Get everything in readineſs."

Here was another peril. To be thrown into the power of a man engaged in illicit traffic, who might eaſily be tempted to betray the truſt which had been forced upon him, was a painful ſituation; but there was no remedy. Notwithſtanding the dangers which ſurrounded me, I embarked the ſecond time in high ſpirits, and was brought in a very ſmall,

ſmall veſſel into the river Weſer. The ſhallows on either ſide afforded the only chance of a ſafe landing; but there were guards at every ſpot that allowed the approach of the ſmalleſt boat. It was poſſible, indeed, that by wading up to the middle for five or ſix miles, one might reach the land unobſerved; but I had neither health nor ſtrength for this mode of travelling. It was at laſt determined that my contrabandiſt guardian ſhould himſelf firſt go aſhore in this manner, and prepare the way for bringing up his veſſel and landing his goods and paſſenger. The ſmack continued its courſe up the river after ſetting him, not, indeed, aſhore, but on his legs in the ſhallow water. In the courſe of the day the crew obſerved a revenue cutter bearing down upon them. The ſkipper, not underſtanding

ing his inſtructions properly, was panic-ſtricken. Haſtily tacking about, he ſteered out to ſea under full ſail, and was in vain hailed and purſued by the cutter. The latter now fired a muſket as a ſignal, which our ſkipper miſtook for a gun, and gave himſelf up for loſt. His veſſel, however, proved the better ſailer, and having fairly outrun and loſt ſight of the cutter he ventured, as night drew on, to drop anchor and await the event. All was quiet till about two o'clock in the morning, when our timorous commander was informed that a boat was rowing along-ſide of us. He came at once to rouſe me from the deep ſlumber in which I lay, and very ſeriouſly bad me prepare for death. It is not improbable that at this juncture the crew would have made a ſecond Jonah of their paſſenger to ſave themſelves, had there

there been time for ſuch a ſtep. When I came on deck I perceived that all this alarm had been occaſioned by the approach of two unarmed men. Theſe proved to be friends too, ſent from the cutter to protect the ſmack, the whole having been ſo adroitly managed by the contraband trader, with the aid of a well-filled purſe, that the very men who had been hired, or rather impreſſed, by the French to guard the coaſts, were ready to aſſiſt him in his traffic. An explanation having taken place, to the no ſmall gratification of the ſkipper and crew, the two men were welcomed moſt cordially, and partook of the beſt cheer on board the ſmack. By the direction of the new comers, we reſumed our former courſe. On coming along-ſide the revenue veſſel, it was decided by a general vote that the moſt obnoxious

part

part of our cargo—myſelf, to wit—ſhould be put on board of her. To this I willingly ſubmitted; but a ſecond boat now making its appearance, renewed our former fears, and I was compelled to make a hurried retreat to my ſtifling berth in the little cabin. We found, however, that our new viſitors were like the firſt, friendly aſſiſtants ſent to us by the worthy free trader; and in the courſe of the following night both veſſels landed their merchandize and paſſenger under the very guns of a fort garriſoned by the French. Whether the ſentinel on duty here was aſleep, or found it his intereſt to appear ſo, he can beſt tell; but ſo it was that the landing took place without ſalute of either gun or muſket; and I was brought to the very houſe which the Chef de la Douane had choſen for his head quarters.

quarters. Doubtleſs Engliſh guineas had preſſed ſo heavily on his eyelids that he needs muſt ſleep on. Not ſo the good ſmuggler, who had found a harbour under the ſame roof, for the moment he was called out of his ſlumbers he ordered horſes to be put to and drove away with his charge. It was to his own houſe that he brought me, and there he entertained me for three days. This time was needed to concert meaſures with other friends by whoſe aid I was to be forwarded on my journey. A communication was opened with a friendly merchant, who agreed not only to receive me, which he did moſt cordially, but to eſcort me in his chariot to the neareſt city, Bremen. It was arranged that another merchant who reſided there ſhould take a drive out of the town, at a certain hour, accompanied, as if for an

Chap. II. 1808.

an airing, by his principal clerk, and that he ſhould meet us at an appointed ſpot. This plan was carried into effect; the carriages met and the clerk reſigned his ſeat to me. There was little reaſon to fear that any queſtions would be aſked at the gates of the town as we entered, ſince two gentlemen had come out, and two would return by the ſame vehicle, which being an open one, rendered us leſs liable to ſuſpicion. Accordingly we drove in without moleſtation.

Chapter

Chapter III.

The too-inquiſitive Hoſt. A Paſſport procured by ſtratagem. Inconvenience of a newly-borrowed Name. Arrival at Hamburg. Incidents in that City and its Neighbourhood. Departure for Lübeck.

Y new hoſt had prepared an excellent dinner, but he plied me ſo hard with wine, and queſtioned me ſo pertinaciouſly about my miſſion, that I was not at all at my eaſe in his ſociety. His inquiſitiveneſs, in fact, exceeded the meaſure of his hoſpitality, and he was evidently not a little vexed at

Chap. III. 1808.

at the taciturnity of his gueſt. I ſoon diſcovered that ſelf-intereſt was the mainſpring of his actions; he had hoped that through my recommendation he might connect himſelf with the Commiſſariat of any body of troops that we might be about to land on theſe coaſts; but when he found that he could neither elicit the information nor obtain the promiſe he deſired, and that his newly raiſed hopes of money-making were not likely to be realized, he loſt his temper, and told me that, ſince I did not chooſe to put confidence in him, I need not any longer expect to be accommodated under his roof. This was an unexpected blow which, but for the clerk who dined with us and witneſſed the unreaſonable conduct of his employer, might have been of ſerious conſequence. The clerk, however, gave me the wink, and, taking

taking leave at the ſame time as myſelf, brought me to a reſpectable hotel, where I paſſed the night.

While I was meditating on various plans of operation, a ſtratagem ſuggeſted itſelf which, at variance, as it doubtleſs was, with the ſtrict rule of veracity, ſeemed allowable, conſidering the object it was to ſerve, and the emergency in which it was adopted. Among my German acquaintances in London there was one nearly of my own age. He had left his native country when a child and never ſince reviſited it. I recollected the place of his birth, and knew that all his relatives were long ſince dead. His name, therefore, I adopted, and, to complete the transformation, I wrote to the prieſt of the pariſh in which the German was born, intimating that after a lapſe of many years Mr. R. was deſirous of viſiting the

the place of his birth, and requeſting that a certificate of his baptiſm, extracted from the pariſh regiſter, might be ſent to him. The prieſt did not heſitate to comply. The atteſtation of birth and baptiſm, ſigned and ſealed in due form, was promptly tranſmitted to me; and this document, coupled with my perfect knowledge of the dialect of that province, completed my Germanization. I did not immediately become poſſeſſed of it, for time was too precious to wait its arrival in Bremen; I therefore left directions to have it ſent after me to Hamburg.

The following day I prevailed on the merchant's clerk to apply at the Town Houſe for a paſſport, as if for a friend who had come from the country on his way to Hamburg. This was granted without difficulty, but it was neceſſary that I ſhould make

make my appearance and ſign my name; and ſuch is the force of habit that I began with the initial letter of my real name, J, which the town-clerk obſerving, ſuddenly called out to me—"How, ſir! did you not tell me your name was Adam?" It was really an unpardonable blunder, and might have proved fatal but for one of the luckieſt thoughts that ever occurred to me in a moment of difficulty. "Sir," I replied (and, certainly, with ſome embarraſſment), "in the palatinate of Bavaria where I was born, we are in the habit of affixing Johann (John) to every man's baptiſmal name, as we do Mary to every woman's, ſo that we do not ſay George, Peter, Adam, &c. but Hans George, Hans Peter, or Hans Adam."* This is really the

* *Hans* is the familiar appellation for Johann.

the caſe. The explanation had the air of truth, and ſaved me for this time. The paſſport, to make it valid, was afterwards to be *viſé* by the French Reſident. The fee, however, was all he wanted, and this point of form being obſerved, little curioſity was evinced concerning the character or deſtination of the traveller. Indeed the natives were ſo hoſtile to the French that the Reſident thought it beſt to pocket his dollars quietly.

One great object was now attained, the firſt town on my route, garriſoned by the French and Dutch, acknowledged the authenticity of my paſſport, and no obſtacle prevented my reaching Hamburg. I preferred travelling by what is called Extra Poſt,—which is, an open waggon drawn by two horſes. By being alone I avoided many impertinent interrogatories, went on more ſpeedily

ily than by any other conveyance, and was treated with more reſpect. When about half-way between Bremen and Hamburg, however, I picked up a companion, who not only leſſened my expenſes, but was of real ſervice by giving me much valuable information. On the ſecond day I reached the banks of the Elbe, oppoſite Hamburg; here my paſſport was inſpected, and on croſſing the river my luggage was ſtrictly examined by the French douaniers. I took up my quarters in a very good hotel, where every deſirable attention was paid to me; but where, nevertheleſs, I ſoon became aware that I was viewed with ſuſpicion. I was provided with a letter of credit on a merchant of great reſpectability. The writing was inviſible to thoſe unaware of the ſecret, and the paper was ſtitched into my pocket-book. On preſenting

presenting it, the person to whom it was directed, having perused its contents, paid the amount specified without the least hesitation ; but while doing so, though he asked no questions, he hinted that the order must be on account of the English Government, and that I must be entrusted with some mission of importance. As I was obliged to make inquiries of some one, I chose rather to hazard a question where confidence had already been reposed, than expose myself to persons who were still greater strangers to me. "Sir," said I, "you have been so prompt in honouring this draft that I need not fear to put one confidential question to you. Be so good as to inform me where is the main body of the Spanish army, under the command of La Romana?" "Oh," replied the German, "I guess your design. What, do do you ſuppoſe you can outwit Bonaparte? Let me tell you he is too many for you." "We can never know unleſs we try," I anſwered. "Try! That has been ſufficiently tried already. I know of three or four who have attempted to reach the army: they and their papers were ſeized, and I need not allude to their fate." "Truly no great encouragement," I obſerved, "yet, try I muſt, and will. I can die but once." "That muſt be as you pleaſe, ſir, let me only beg of you not to return to my houſe; I have no ambition to be ſhot or hanged on your account. Romana is at Nyborg, in the Iſle of Fünen, a long way from here. Be aſſured you will never reach him. It was only the other day that the probability of the Marquis's evaſion was diſcuſſed at a public dinner; ſome of the gueſts held

CHAP. III.
1808.

held it to be a likely event; others ridiculed ſuch a notion; but Bernadotte, who was preſent, pronounced it ſimply an impoſſibility." "Sir," ſaid I, "you have it no doubt in your power to convey intelligence to Romana: as a merchant you have correſpondence in every direction. Would you be kind enough to forward a letter from me through any friend?" "That is what I neither can nor will undertake," anſwered the German. "I have told you where are his head-quarters—it is *your* buſineſs to do the reſt—*mine* not to intermeddle. I have too much property at ſtake. Adieu."

Thus abruptly diſmiſſed, I deliberated as to what was next to be done. On making ſome inquiries I learned that the Spaniards had their hoſpital near Altona, and that the ſick were attended by a prieſt of their own

own nation. Thus informed, I repaired to the Catholic chapel at Altona, and entering the veſtry, requeſted an interview with the prieſt. The German miſſionary firſt preſented himſelf; but I expreſſed a wiſh to ſee his Spaniſh colleague, who accordingly made his appearance, and whom I addreſſed in Latin. I began by ſaying that I felt aſſured a ſecret entruſted to a prieſt and a Spaniard would be held inviolable; the anſwer I received was a diſtinct promiſe to this effect. I then avowed myſelf a clergyman and brother, ſtated that I was charged with a very important communication to the Spaniſh Commander-in-Chief, and requeſted of his kindneſs that he would put me in the way of doing ſo with ſafety. The Caſtilian, candidly confeſſing in the firſt place that he was not in the habit of converſing in Latin,

CHAP. III.

1808.

Latin, replied further that he was quite at a loſs what to adviſe, and propoſed to refer the matter to an invalid officer who could ſpeak French. To this I demurred, intimating that the riſk was too great; but my conductor aſſuring me that the officer of whom he ſpoke was a man of honour, and a patriot, I ſuffered myſelf to be led to him, and again exacting a promiſe of ſecreſy, which he gave on the honour of a Spaniſh cavalier, imparted to him the general purport of my commiſſion, and was liſtened to with great attention. "I congratulate you," ſaid the Spaniard, "on having had ſuch a miſſion confided to you; and I alſo congratulate you on the precaution you have taken of carrying no papers. If Bernadotte himſelf were to call on me now, as he ſometimes does, and find you here, there

is

is no danger for you or me. I do not hold high rank in the army, and have no immediate relation with the Commander-in-Chief. I know not what his conduct may be on this critical occasion: but, were his sentiments such as your Government desires, what could he do without the concurrence of his subordinates? The state of my health prevents my taking an active part either way: all that I can say is, that your secret shall remain buried in my bosom."

"If so, sir, may I at least hope that by your assistance I may get a letter conveyed to your general by some officer or private soldier returning from the hospital here to head quarters?"

"That is a request," replied the captain, "which, from principle, I must refuse. Do you ask me why? consider, sir, if a letter of that tenor were intercepted, the life of the bearer would

CHAP. III.

1808.

would be in imminent jeopardy. How could I aſk any one to carry ſuch a paper, without at leaſt putting him on his guard:—and how could that be done without riſking a betrayal of your ſecret? No, no, ſir, you are the man who undertook the taſk, you are the man to finiſh the work. I wiſh you ſucceſs, but can do nothing to aſſiſt you."

Theſe arguments were too cogent to be controverted. I took leave of my Spaniſh friends and ſet about preparing for the dangerous journey, on the ſucceſs of which my own fate and a train of momentous conſequences depended.

During my ſtay in Hamburg I collected whatever information I could concerning the man to whom I was addreſſed. Romana's character ſtood high in the public opinion at Hamburg. When the Spaniards firſt reached

reached that city, they found the people ſtrongly prejudiced againſt them. They had been repreſented by the malicious French as blood-thirſty bigots, who would be glad of a pretext to deſtroy all Proteſtants. But they had not been long in the place before they gained the love of the inhabitants by their friendly conduct and good diſcipline. The French ridiculed their want of alertneſs on parade; but Romana drew up and circulated printed inſtructions for his officers, which were followed with ſuch alacrity and intelligence, that the Spaniſh troops ſoon ceaſed to be a ſource of mirth to their captious critics.

Great jealouſy exiſted between Bernadotte and the Marquis: the latter could not bear the imperious manner in which he was treated, and boldly reminded Bernadotte that he alſo

Chap. III. 1808.

alſo was a Marſhal,* one of older ſtanding, too, than himſelf, and entitled, therefore, to the reſpect which the junior officer in every rank is bound to pay to his ſenior.

Romana had been for ſome time Governor of Hamburg, a poſt which the French generals who preceded him had turned to good account. They had levied whatever contributions they pleaſed, and lived with their troops at free quarters. One of them (Dupas, I believe) obliged the magiſtrates to furniſh thirty-ſix diſhes

* It does not appear from any biographical notice of La Romana that has fallen in my way that he had in fact attained this exalted military rank. I ſhould conjecture that Mr. Robertſon, or his informant, may have been miſled by the uſe of the French term "maréchal de camp," which a civilian might fancy equivalent to *field-marſhal*, but which, I believe, really means only "major-general."—Ed.

diſhes daily for his table. By this the reader may gueſs what their exactions were in other ways. The principal citizens remonſtrated with Bernadotte, who thought he had left them no ground of complaint, when he reſtricted the Governor to *half* his accuſtomed number of diſhes. Romana's conduct had been exactly the reverſe of that which the French had purſued. When about to quit the place, he was entreated by the citizens to accept of a ſtate-carriage as a mark of their reſpect and gratitude. "No," replied the generous Spaniard, "no, my good people, you have too many burthens to bear already—I will accept no preſent at your hands."

The following anecdote ſets his character in a very amiable light. He had fixed his quarters for ſome time in a manſion belonging to one of of the moſt reſpectable families in the city. One day he ſaid to the lady of the houſe: "I wiſh to make a preſent of ſome value to a young favourite of mine, and it has occurred to me that an aſſortment of ſuch elegancies as Hamburg can ſupply would hardly fail to be acceptable to her. Now, madam, as a ſoldier, I do not underſtand theſe matters: will you have the goodneſs to make a ſelection of this kind for me? Here is a purſe, you will oblige me by expending its contents to the beſt of your judgment. Let it be a liberal equipment in dreſſes and trinkets, and of the firſt faſhion." The lady readily undertook the agreeable taſk, and after many days devoted to its execution, invited the Marquis to inſpect her purchaſes. Nothing could be better choſen, and the Marquis intermingled many compliments on her

her taſte with the thanks which he offered for the trouble ſhe had ſo kindly taken. "But pray have you ſhown all this to your daughter?" "No, indeed, general." "Then oblige me by calling her." The daughter, a girl about thirteen, was enraptured with the finery ſhe ſaw; but how ſhall I convey any notion of her delight when the Marquis added:—"My dear, this is a preſent which your mother makes you."

Such was the man whom Bonaparte hated and dreaded: ſuch was the man to be delivered out of his hands.

I received information here that our Government had offered 200*l.* to any one who would convey to Romana's army the proclamations of the Spaniſh Junta. An individual, whom I will not mention, undertook to do ſo; and on his declaration that he he had accomplifhed the object, obtained the promifed reward. How true his affertion was will appear in the fequel.

Before proceeding further, I deemed it neceffary to apprize Mr. McKenzie of the diftance I had to travel, and of the dangers that lay in my way, in order that more money might be placed at my difpofal. Mr. McKenzie remitted a further fum, and with it fent intelligence of the commencement of the infurrection in Galicia and the Afturias; the names of the deputies from Spain to England; and their reception at court and in the city of London. Having now replenifhed my purfe, I made it my firft care to purchafe a fmall quantity of the beft Havannah cigars and a few pounds of chocolate. My next ftep was to prefent myfelf at the bureau with my Bremen paffport,

port, in order to have it extended to Lübeck, which was conceded without difficulty. I preferred this circuitous route, becauſe it furniſhed no clue to my ultimate deſtination. As a further precaution, I procured letters of introduction to ſeveral merchants, to each of whom I remitted a ſum of money ſufficient to inſure civility at their hands without exciting ſuſpicion. Being thus fully prepared, I departed from Hamburg in a return chaiſe and reached the ſhores of the Baltic in ſafety.

Chapter IV.

The Condition of Lübeck during its Occupation by the French. Difficulties encountered in the Journey between Lübeck and the Isle of Fünen. Arrival at the Head-quarters of La Romana.

HE engagement between the French and the Prussians, under Blücher, soon after the battle of Jena, will long be remembered by the ancient Hanseatic, and once free, city of Lübeck. It had not offended, nor was it subject to, either of the belligerents. Without the power of resistance, it was occupied by the retreating Prussians,

ſians, who were attacked, and after a ſevere cannonading, driven from the town.

The public vehicle which conveyed me to Lübeck carried back thither the lady of one of the citizens, whoſe ſtory was rather ſingular. Their houſe, from its expoſed ſituation, had ſuffered a good deal from the fire of the enemy, and ſtill ſhe remained in it; but when the ſoldiery broke in to plunder, ſhe, though in the laſt ſtage of pregnancy, ruſhed into the ſtreet, where the fright brought on the pains of labour; a number of women formed a circle round her, and there, in the public market-place, under the canopy of heaven, was ſhe delivered of a daughter, with whom ſhe was now returning from Hamburg, where ſhe had been on a viſit to her relations. She aſſured me that the brutal victors ſhowed

Chap. IV.

1808.

ſhowed her no pity even in that awful moment, and that, but for the humanity of one of the officers, ſhe would have fallen a victim to their barbarity. I was politely invited to her houſe, which ſtill bore the marks of the cannon-ſhot, and was entertained by her huſband with great hoſpitality, notwithſtanding the loſſes he had incurred by the war. The harſh and oppreſſive character of the military dominion eſtabliſhed by the French was, in no inſtance, more revoltingly diſplayed than in their behaviour towards this defenceleſs city. To the hour of its final incorporation with the French empire its inhabitants were treated as enemies. Troops were continually quartered on them, and heavy contributions exacted, although they had never attempted reſiſtance, nor taken any voluntary part in the war. Complaints

plaints and remonſtrances were fruitleſs. Though, in conjunction with their neighbours and ancient confederates of Hamburg and Bremen, they ſent deputation after deputation to Napoleon to ſue for more lenient treatment, the rigour of his yoke was not relaxed. Such was the condition of the once free and imperial city at the date of my viſit.

The merchants to whom I had addreſſes for credit or advice waited on me, and freely offered their ſervices. When I mentioned my deſign of proceeding as far as Copenhagen, they expreſſed great ſurpriſe, and one and all aſſured me that no conſideration would tempt them to venture ſo far, as the Engliſh veſſels of war were ſwarming in the adjacent ſeas. I liſtened with feigned ſolicitude to their warnings, but ſignified that the profits of the adventure I had

Chap. IV. 1808.

had in view would more than compensate for its perils. The only favour I had to ask of them was to procure me a passport from the Danish consul,—a service which was readily and successfully undertaken.

During my stay at Lübeck I formed an intimacy with a good-hearted Italian who had forsaken his country when he found it invaded by the French, and had since travelled a great deal. From him I learned the following anecdote of Canova. Bonaparte said one day to the artist:—"Canova, I want you to make a statue for me." "Of whom?" inquired the other. "Of Liberty," said Napoleon. "Liberty!" exclaimed the sculptor; "am I to represent her alive or dead?"

After one day spent in making the necessary arrangements, I took my departure for the Danish dominions

in

in a poſt-chaiſe, ſuch as the country affords. Nothing worth recording occurred till I reached Kiel, a handſome town, near which the King of Denmark has a reſidence, where the court happened to be when the Engliſh took Copenhagen. On entering the town the uſual queſtions were aſked, but my paſſport was not examined. I learned that there was a veſſel lying in the river, bound for Aroë, one of the Daniſh iſlands; and immediately proceeding to the quay, I hailed the ſhip and was taken on board without heſitation. Kiel is beautifully ſituated on a large navigable river which, a few miles below the town, empties itſelf into the Baltic, while, by means of an excellent canal, it communicates with Tonningen on the German Ocean. The Medical College has ſome repute, and the Botanic Garden is worth notice.

CHAP. IV.
1808.

notice. The royal country ſeat, where the queen then was, is but a ſhort diſtance from Kiel.

One tide brought our veſſel to the mouth of the river, where we anchored under the guns of a well-conſtructed fort. Here the maſter delayed for nearly two days, pretending fear of the Engliſh, who were cruiſing in the Belt. To my anxious inquiries when he would get under weigh, I received for an anſwer that it was very doubtful when the coaſt would be clear. It was eaſy to perceive that what he really was in doubt about was the character of his paſſenger. He ſaid we muſt firſt be viſited by the garriſon of the fort, and begged I would not expoſe myſelf and him, if I had any reaſon to be afraid. He aſſured me, beſides, that we ſhould run great riſk at landing, as he was not

authoriſed

authorised to bring strangers into the country.

I was prevailed on at length to return to Kiel, and to proceed further up by land. A wherry passing up the river took me from the vessel, which, the moment I left it, set sail and proceeded on her voyage. A short hour brought me to Kiel, where I took post without delay. From the driver of my chaise, an intelligent man, I learned that by crossing over to the Isle of Assens, I might save both time and money: besides which, I should travel with less publicity. The peasantry in the north of Germany and in Denmark accommodate travellers with horses and waggons nearly as good as the post-chaises, and much cheaper. They are, indeed, restricted from forwarding those who arrive by post, for the first day after their arrival. This regulation

Chap. IV.

1808.

regulation can, however, be evaded. The driver propoſed to carry me to a good farm-houſe a little off the poſt-road, where he aſſured me I ſhould find comfortable accommodation, and might hire the farmer's car to carry me to the coaſt. The advice was adopted, and one day more brought me to a retired ſpot on the little Belt, where I hired for a dollar a very good paſſage-boat which landed me at Aſſens. This ſmall iſland, about three miles broad, is ſeparated from the continent by a very narrow ſtrait, and from Fünen by another arm of the Baltic ſcarcely two hours' ſail acroſs. Immediately on landing I entered the town and lighted on a good inn and coffee-houſe, from which poſting was expedited, and where the officer lodged who commanded a party of military in the place. Here it was neceſſary

to

to produce the paſſport; and an objection was made that it had not been inſpected and marked ſince my entrance into the Daniſh dominions. I explained that this was owing to no fault of mine, but to the neglect of the functionaries, who had never called for it. I added that I had choſen a ſhort route to avoid expenſe. Luckily, the officer, happening to be a Hanoverian who had entered the ſervice of Denmark, was ſo delighted at hearing the lateſt news from his own country, that he at once admitted my excuſe.

Here I made a ſhow of taking orders for various articles, ſuch as wines, cigars, &c., from the poſtmaſter and inn-keeper. Theſe orders ſerved afterwards as proofs that the purpoſe of my journey was commercial ſpeculation. The drive acroſs the little iſland was the work of that evening.

Chap. IV. 1808.

evening. I paſſed the night at a tolerable inn at the ferry, where a bureau is kept for the inſpection of paſſports, and a guard-houſe to prevent ſmuggling. Three men rowed the boat acroſs next morning, and ſafely conveyed me to my land of promiſe, the Iſland of Fünen.

This was the principal ſtation of the Spaniſh troops; and the inn to which I was conducted, on landing, proved to be the quarters of one of their colonels. A bed was found for me with difficulty. Next morning I was received politely by the old colonel, who was very deaf, but, fortunately for me, by no means dumb or uncommunicative. He readily imparted all he knew of the army, that the dealer in chocolate and cigars might know exactly where to find the cuſtomers of whom he was in queſt. He ſtated that the Spaniſh contingent

contingent had conſiſted originally of 18,000 men, but deſertion, fatigue, and diſeaſe had diminiſhed its numbers conſiderably during the two years or more which had elapſed ſince it quitted Spain. He enumerated all the regiments and their reſpective ſtations, complained much of his own wretched quarters and hard uſage: ſpoke deſpondingly of his failing health, and murmured at being kept in ignorance of the fate of his country.

He confirmed the intelligence that the Commander-in-Chief was at Nyborg with his ſtaff. Thus inſtructed, I ſet out on my laſt day's journey, which brought me to the ſpot where the great purpoſe of my perilous miſſion was to be achieved or baffled, the head-quarters of the Marquis de la Romana.

Chapter

CHAPTER V.

The Long-ſought Interview obtained. La Romana made acquainted with the Propoſal of the Britiſh Government.

Chap. V.
1808.

YBORG is a fortified harbour and neat town on the Belt. Between it and Zealand were lying ſeveral Engliſh ſhips of war which kept both ſides ſtrictly blockaded; yet at different times 3,000 Spaniards, availing themſelves of the opportunities which the changes of wind and weather afforded them, had ſafely effected a tranſit to the oppoſite coaſt. About 8,000 remained

remained in Fünen, diſperſed through its ſeveral towns.

It was about midnight when the carriage drove up to the beſt inn of the town. The ſeaſon being midſummer, there was no darkneſs in this northern climate. The town-gates had been readily opened to us for a ſmall fee; but the landlord of the hotel excuſed himſelf from admitting me on the plea that his houſe was quite full of Spaniards, the greater part of it being occupied by the General and his retinue. I urged in reply that his houſe had been ſpecially recommended to me, and begged him to admit me in any way or on any terms. He then ſaid there was not a room in the houſe in which I could be accommodated except one which he occupied himſelf, but that, if I pleaſed, he would put a ſecond bed for me there. I cloſed

Chap. V.

1808.

cloſed with his offer the more readily as it ſeemed to me that in ſuch a nook I ſhould be all the more likely to eſcape obſervation. On my admiſſion I ordered a good ſupper, and engaged the landlord to take his ſhare with me of a very excellent bottle of wine, which encouraged converſation. I learned that the Marquis kept a numerous retinue and a good table, having two cooks and two *valets-de-chambre*, beſides livery-ſervants: and, moreover, that he was a man of affable manners, and much beloved. A meſſage delivered through one of his ſervants, the landlord ſaid, would eaſily procure acceſs to him, which might probably be followed by orders of goods for his army. Accordingly, next morning, after breakfaſt, I wrote in French to this effect:—

That a foreign merchant (*négociant*

viant étranger) deſired to have the honour of a private interview with his Excellency the Commander-in-Chief, in order to preſent to him ſamples of ſome articles he dealt in, and to ſolicit from his Excellency facilities for the proſecution of his further journey.

To prevent ſuſpicion this note was ſent open by the French valet, who returned immediately with a favourable reply. I took a box of my beſt cigars under my arm, and a few pounds of chocolate in my hand, and followed the Frenchman upſtairs, not a little agitated, and doubtful of the event.

In an elegant ſaloon, through which I had to paſs, were ſeated ſeveral general officers, *aides-de-camp*, and others, who eyed me ſtedfaſtly, then looked at each other ſignificantly, and again meaſured me from

head

head to foot. I underwent this ocular ſcrutiny with conſcious embarraſſment, which increaſed when I found myſelf in the adjoining chamber. The Marquis was rather low of ſtature, but he had an air of dignity, and a look which beſpoke deep penetration and cool reflection. His manner was diſtant at firſt, yet without any of that repulſive *hauteur* which is attributed to his countrymen. I was no ſooner cloſeted with the illuſtrious grandee than I thus began my faltering ſpeech :

" Señor, you ſee before you a ſtranger who comes to put his life in your hands. I am a Catholic prieſt, choſen, perhaps, partly on that account for the miſſion I am about to explain, as it was imagined that a Spaniard might be diſpoſed to put confidence in the word of a Catholic clergyman. I am directed to your Excellency

Excellency by the English Government; but let me say at once, I have no papers whatsoever to deliver to you, so that, in the event of my being arrested, you cannot be compromised in the least degree; and, moreover, I desire no writing from you. My message is merely verbal; be your answer the same. All that I can offer in the way of credentials is the knowledge I have of certain particulars of your personal intercourse with Mr. Frere, whom you will remember as our Ambassador in Spain. He desires me to remind your Excellency that the first time he had the pleasure of dining with you was at Toledo. After dinner you withdrew together into a cabinet containing books. In this cabinet there was one picture. That picture was by Mengs, and represented St. Peter and St. John at the gate of the

the Temple." "All most true," exclaimed the General, his countenance assuming the most friendly aspect. "Would your Excellency recognise Mr. Frere's handwriting?" I continued. "Methinks I should!" Here I produced a very small fragment torn from a memorandum I had received from Mr. Frere, which was immediately recognised by the Marquis. Having thus established my credit as a confidential agent of the British Government, I added that "Mr. Frere had assured me I should find in the General a man of strict honour and high principle, and an enemy to French tyranny and oppression.

"The message," I continued, "with which I am charged, is to announce to your Excellency that England is ready to convey you and the troops under your command to any

any country you may name. We ask nothing of you in return; you shall be free from any engagement to fight for us; in that respect act as you think proper. We simply wish to put it in your power to extricate yourself from your present position. Our transports shall attend your orders on any part of the coast. You may select South America, or Canada, Minorca, England, or Spain as your destination; we are ready to forward your views, whatever they may be. If you desire a treaty in form, the British Government has authorised Mr. McKenzie to conclude one with you. He resides at Heligoland at present, and will there treat with any officer you may depute.

"Further, although we do not pretend to dictate to the Spanish nation what course it ought to pursue, yet if resistance to the invader be be reſolved on, we are ready to co-operate with all our might. Our cavalry were never better mounted, nor our artillery better ſerved. We long for an opportunity to try our ſtrength on land with the French."

Having delivered my meſſage without any interruption on the part of the General, I pauſed. But finding the Spaniard not inclined to break ſilence, I, for a moment, trembled for my own ſafety. "Is he," thought I, "ſo weak that he ſhrinks from any ſhow of difficulty?—then he may be wicked enough to ſell my life to Bonaparte, merely to give him a proof of his fidelity." "General," ſaid I, in ſome agitation, "need I feel a doubt that I have idly repoſed confidence in the honour of a Spaniſh Cavalier?" "Sir," anſwered the Marquis, in an impreſſive tone, "you have nothing to fear from me! But

have

have you mentioned your errand to any one ſince your arrival on the Continent?" "I have, Señor, of neceſſity. Our Miniſtry could not inform me where you were quartered: they ſuppoſed you in garriſon at Glückſtadt on the Elbe. I firſt addreſſed myſelf to one of your prieſts who attends the ſick. I bound him to ſecreſy; from him, I am convinced, there is nothing to be apprehended. He introduced me to one of your officers, who aſſured me he would ſooner die than reveal my ſecret. He has been faithful to his word, otherwiſe I ſhould not be here." "I aſk you again," rejoined the Marquis, "are theſe the only perſons in whom you have confided?" "I recollect one more—one to whom I preſented a letter of credit, and who gueſſed my buſineſs the moment I inquired where your Excellency

Chap. V. 1808.

Excellency was to be found." "I am ſorry for it," replied the General. "So am I, my Lord, ſince you view the circumſtance in that light; but will you be pleaſed to conſider, that the perſon alluded to enjoys the confidence of our Miniſtry, otherwiſe I ſhould not have been referred to him. I know he has too much property at ſtake in both countries to commit himſelf. I have reaſon, however, to complain, if after having refuſed to tranſmit to your Excellency a letter which I would have committed to his charge, he has been ſo officious as to acquaint you underhand with the nature of my miſſion. Will your Excellency now permit me to aſk whether any other agent from the Britiſh Government has anticipated me, and eſpecially whether any of the declarations of the Spaniſh nation have reached your army? I

aſk

ask this because a person whose domicile is on the Continent claims the credit of having conveyed those declarations to your quarters, and has actually received the reward which was offered for that service." "Be assured," replied the Marquis, "there is no truth in his assertion. If any such papers had been dispersed among my troops, they could not have escaped my notice. Yours is the first and only communication of this kind that has reached me either from England or from Spain."

"Well then, General; may I beg the favour of an answer to my principal? I have the means of forwarding it to Mr. McKenzie, and to London." "An answer—what now? surely you will not depart immediately!" "Certainly not, my Lord; though I came at the peril of my life, and remain at the same risk, I shall

Chap. V.

1808.

ſhall not take my departure to-day."
"Then we ſhall meet again?"
"Whenever your Excellency pleaſes. I have a ſtock of choice cigars and chocolate for ſale, which may furniſh a pretext for a ſecond interview."

Chapter

CHAPTER VI.

Second Conference with the Spaniſh General. Promiſing, though not concluſive, indications of his diſpoſition to accept the Offer made him on the part of England.

Y firſt converſation with La Romana ended in the manner I have related. Having diſburthened my mind, the load of merchandize felt much lighter in my hand. Below I encountered a moſt inquiſitive Jew, whoſe queſtions I anſwered very laconically. Pretending buſineſs, I ſauntered out through the town, and on my return to the hotel found the windows over the gateway

Chap. VI.
1808.

gateway occupied by the General and his officers. The moment I was obſerved to enter the houſe, a ſummons was brought down by the French valet for the man with the cigars. As I paſſed through the ſaloon the ſecond time, a very viſible alteration ſtruck me: every face now beamed a friendly welcome. On my part, I could not entirely diſguiſe the feelings by which I was agitated. On re-entering the Marquis' cabinet, I ſaid, "I preſume, General, I ſhall now have the honour of your reply?" "Sir," ſaid he, "before I decide on your propoſition, let me obſerve that we are utterly ignorant of what is going on in Spain. For a whole year, not one letter has been ſuffered to reach us. We know no more than the French chooſe to tell us in the public papers. In ſuch intelligence we can put no truſt. One of their

their fabrications is the reported death of your king on the 4th of June last."

"As to the affairs of Spain, General, you shall know through me whatever is known in England. And first, I have to inform you, that the insurrection has already commenced in Galicia and the Asturias. Already has a deputation arrived in London to solicit the aid and protection of our Government. The names of the Deputies* are Don Antonio —, Don

CHAP. VI. 1808.

* It would appear that at the time when Mr. Robertson reduced this narrative to writing, his memory had failed him a little as to the names of these Deputies. From *Toreno's* "*Historia del Levantamiento de España*," we learn that the Deputies from the Asturias (who landed at Falmouth on the 6th of June, 1808) were the author himself, Don José Maria de Llano, then Vizconde de Matarrosa, afterwards Conde de Toreno, and Don Andres Angel de la Vega; and that the Deputy from Galicia (who arrived in England a few days later) was Don Francisco Sangro.

Don Josef de —, Don Pedro —." "How!" interrupted the Marquis, "these are men I know well; men of the highest influence in the country." "So much the better, my Lord, you best can say whether they are men of honour and principle." "They are, indeed!" he replied. "I rejoice to hear it," I rejoined, "for I conclude the Commander-in-Chief of the Spanish troops in Denmark will be of one mind with such men." "They would have us believe," observed the General, "that there was a universal jubilee in Spain at the arrival of Joseph there. But we are little disposed to credit such a tale. Still, what can I do, situated as I am at present? My troops are dispersed through all the provinces and islands of Denmark. In Seeland there are 8,000 men, 2,000 in Langeland; some

ſome are in Jutland, others in Sleſwick: had the Engliſh not blockaded the Belt we might all have been in Seeland, and then we might have attempted ſomething." "If it be not too late," I replied, "our Government, I doubt not, will act on the ſlighteſt intimation of your wiſh, and leave your paſſage to Seeland unobſtructed." "That would be attended with too much *éclat*," remarked the General. "Well, Señor, if you cannot reſcue all, reſcue at leaſt what portion of your force you can."

"Alas! to what purpoſe?" anſwered the Marquis; "what can we —what can Spain do againſt France? Never did Europe groan under ſuch a ſlavery. Liberty ſtill finds a refuge in England, it is true; but even England, that laſt remaining bulwark againſt the Uſurper, is not exempt

CHAP. VI.
1808.

empt from danger, while ſo much diſcontent prevails in Ireland, and while your Government demurs about granting to the Catholics equal rights with their fellow-ſubjects. What is not to be dreaded in that vulnerable part of the Britiſh dominions? And, if Britain fall, who ſhall ſtand?" "General, as to the ſtate of Ireland, I might be prepared to anſwer you. I have but lately left that country, where I ſpent ſome years; and, more recently, I have liſtened to the debates on Catholic Emancipation in both Houſes of Parliament. As a Catholic, I muſt regret with your Excellency the unjuſt delay of that meaſure, the conceſſion of which would, no doubt, ſtrengthen our common cauſe. But during the reign of George III. much has been done for the benefit of the Catholics, and they are not ungrateful

ungrateful for it; what remains to be conceded will come in progreſs of time: any inſurrectionary movement would infallibly retard that epoch; any ſervice we can render the State ought to accelerate it, and ſurely will. We have no fear," I continued, "for the preſent, either of rebellion at home or invaſion from abroad; the diſgraceful ſupineneſs and paſſive ſubmiſſion of other countries, conſtitute our chief difficulty." "But the reſt of Europe does nothing?" "Throughout the greater part of Europe, General, the indignant feeling of the people is held in reſtraint by their rulers,—by princes unworthy of their ſtation, who, to preſerve a ſhadowy ſemblance of royal dignity for themſelves and their families, are content to ſacrifice their own honour and the welfare of their ſubjects. So they accept

accept their condition of vaſſalage, while a miſtaken ſentiment of allegiance paralyſes the reſiſtance of their ſubjects, even when handed over to a foreign Deſpot. Your nation is at liberty to act for itſelf. Your Sovereigns exiſt no more for you. To you it is that Europe muſt look for a great example. Who knows what it may produce? 'Already Auſtria is prepared to ſtrike the blow. If you command, I will at once repair to the Arch-Duke Charles, appriſe him of your ſentiments, and point out to him that his duty and intereſt alike require he ſhould boldly eſpouſe the cauſe of a country over which he, in default of the dethroned Bourbons, has the beſt right to reign." On this the Marquis made ſome very pertinent remarks. He ſeemed much to wiſh that a Regent ſhould be appointed immediately,

immediately, one, if possible, of the blood-royal, with a council of Regency to assist him in the Government. He recommended that every exertion should be used to prevent Bonaparte from attacking South America, or the other dependencies of Spain. He stated the exact number of troops necessary to occupy Minorca and the other Baleares, &c. I expressed the fullest confidence that the Spanish-American territories, with all their resources, would be effectually protected from the ambition of the Usurper, and that we should eventually be able to wrest the whole of Spain from his grasp.

This interesting interview was frequently interrupted by the intrusive entrance of the French valet. As often as he appeared, the conversation turned on the cigars and the chocolate

Chap. VI.

1808.

late. When we were left alone the Marquis remarked that he was surrounded by spies, and could not be too circumspect. In conclusion, he said, he should require some time to collect and prepare his officers and men for embarkation. He would not pledge himself to anything. He had not been asked, and he was not inclined, to give any written answer to the proposal I had conveyed to him; neither would he promise to correspond with me at Hamburg, though he took a note of my address in that city. I requested to know whether he could in any way help me to get on board any English vessel off the coast. His answer was, of necessity, in the negative. To attempt this might endanger the success of the whole undertaking. But he seemed to think it might be practicable for me to escape the vigilance of of the Danish sentinels who guarded the coast. Elated with this hope I took my leave. Chap. VI. 1808.

Chapter VII.

Fruitleſs attempt to communicate with the Engliſh Fleet. Arreſt, and ſubſequent diſmiſſal. The Hoſt's Suſpicions diſarmed. Final Interview with La Romana, who cloſes with the Propoſal of the Britiſh Government.

Chap. VII. 1808.

N quitting the Marquis I repaired to the ſhore, within ſight of the town, and of the Engliſh fleet. I ſauntered about on the beach with a ſmall linen bag in my hand, filling it, leiſurely, with the pebbles and ſhells which I gathered, and occaſionally caſting away a portion of my ſtock for ſome new acquiſition

acquisition that seemed to please me better. Ever and anon I took out a white handkerchief, which I waved, as if by accident, in the hope of being descried from the fleet. I had walked some distance along the shore, and had succeeded in attracting the notice of the English; but, alas! to little purpose; for at the moment I thought a boat was putting off for me, I was observed by a Danish militia-man, who lay couched on the grass, with his musket beside him. There was no retreating. I saw that my safety depended solely on my self-possession. Accordingly I stepped up to the man and greeted him in German. I congratulated Denmark on having such vigilant protectors against their faithless enemies (pointing to the fleet), and inquired how I might manage to get across the Belt, without falling into the hands of the English.

Chap. VII. 1808.

Engliſh. In ſpite of the beſt countenance I could put on, the Dane eyed me very ſuſpiciouſly, but recommended me to addreſs myſelf to a fiſherman who was the owner of ſeveral boats, and who lived in the next cottage. Hither, accordingly, I proceeded; but while treating with the boatman, ſix ſturdy Danes ruſhed in with fixed bayonets, and preſenting their weapons to my breaſt, demanded, with menacing geſtures, who I was. As often as memory reverts to this incident, I am compelled to wonder at the preſence of mind and compoſure of manner with which I was gifted by a gracious Providence at that perilous moment, when both were ſo needful to my ſafety. Conſcious that the leaſt appearance of timidity would betray me, I raiſed my heart to God, begging to be fortified, and calmly replied:

plied: "I am a merchant." "Have you a passport?" "Certainly:" I answered. "Show it!" "Here it is!" It was in German, and not one of the party could read it. They, of course, condemned it as not good. "Why not good?" said I; "don't you know the arms of your king? Look at this seal." "No, it won't do," was the reply. "Where do you come from?" "From Nyborg." "We will conduct you back to Nyborg." "That as you please," I replied; "but as I found my way hither along the shore, I cannot mistake my way back again." "We will take care you shall not: come along with us."

When I left the cottage, thus escorted, the sight drew the attention of the whole village, and some hundreds of people crowded round to express their indignation at the audacity

Chap. VII.

1808.

dacity of the intruder, and their ſpiteful joy at his capture. One young girl among the reſt preſſed anxiouſly forward to have a gaze at the priſoner, and to her I jocoſely held out my hand in token of friendſhip. But no common felon, no murderer, was ever treated with greater ſcorn than I was for my miſplaced gallantry. The repulſive geſture of the damſel did not in the leaſt diſcompoſe me, but, on the contrary, ſerved as a good diverſion, and produced, very ſeaſonably, a hearty and general burſt of laughter. The ſoldiers knew not what to do with their prize. Firſt they queſtioned me cloſely, and then they offered me a glaſs of brandy, but ſtill nothing could be gathered from my words or looks. In a ſhort time they reached another village, where the Serjeant of the party was quartered. To him they reported

reported the prisoner they had made, expecting, no doubt, much praise for their achievement. This Serjeant turned out to be a very honest-hearted Hanoverian.

Leaving the party in the kitchen, he led me into his own apartment, and accosted me in good German: "What the devil," said he, "tempted you to throw yourself into the hands of these fellows?" "Do not be uneasy on my account, sir," I replied, "I have not the least cause for fear." "Have you a passport, then?" "Undoubtedly." "Let me look at it. Why, this is a very excellent passport: but why did they arrest you?" "Because they cannot read." "I am the more sorry for their mistake," rejoined the Serjeant, "because I have not authority to rectify it. Being only a subaltern, I cannot release any one brought to me

Chap. VII.

1808.

me as a priſoner." "So I conceive," ſaid I; "but what do you intend to do with me?" "I muſt tranſport (eſcort) you." "Tranſport me! Whither, I pray?" "To Nyborg." "That I rejoice to hear," ſaid I. "My goods and luggage are left there at my lodgings." "At what houſe?" "At the firſt hotel." "I beg pardon, ſir, none but gentlemen of diſtinction frequent that houſe." "And I generally frequent the company of gentlemen. But, my good Serjeant," I continued, "I have one favour to aſk. You know it would be very vexatious, and not very creditable to a gentleman and a merchant to be marched publicly into the town, eſcorted like a criminal, by ſix of your countrymen well armed. You can ſave me that diſgrace; come with me yourſelf. I am an old man, and cannot run from you: weapons

I

I have none but this walking-stick; if you are afraid of it I will throw it away. Take what arms you please, but be you my only escort." "Agreed," replied the friendly Serjeant; let me dismiss my men, and I will attend you."

The party went off, accordingly, not a little disappointed: and the good Hanoverian, girding on his sabre, set forth with his charge.

After we had left the village, the Serjeant proposed to wait on his Colonel, whose country-seat was but a short distance off the direct road to Nyborg. "If you have no objection," he said, "to be presented to him, I have little doubt but he will set you at liberty, which I could not take on myself to do." I, of course, gladly acceded to his proposal, and in a short time we reached the Colonel's residence. We found him engaged

Chap. VII.
1808.

engaged with a ſmall party at a game of nine-pins, or ſkittles. He was a very young man, and remarkably polite. He examined my paſſports, and found them all perfectly regular. "Sir," ſaid he, "I am, indeed, very ſorry that the ſoldiers under my command ſhould have cauſed you ſo much uneaſineſs and trouble; your paſſports are quite ſatisfactory. But my men are ſo ignorant, they cannot read German; and you ſee we are beſet by enemies on all ſides: no wonder we ſhould look on every ſtrange face with ſuſpicion. For theſe reaſons I hope you will excuſe the treatment you have met with, and conſole yourſelf with the reflection that you have ſeen a very pleaſant part of the country." "Sir," I replied, "if your country is a pleaſant one, it is the more worthy of ſuch inhabitants as yourſelf. And

as

as for your men, they have only done their duty. I give them credit for it, and rejoice to see that your coast is so watchfully guarded." "My men and their Colonel are obliged to you, sir, for your good opinion. I have the honour," he continued, "to wish you a good evening: you are at perfect liberty, sir, to depart when you please, and proceed in what direction you will."

I thanked him politely for his kindness, and, rejoicing not a little in such an issue to the adventure, took leave of the good-natured Hanoverian, and returned, much fatigued in body and mind, to my inn at Nyborg. On my arrival my worthy host, with whom I had previously been on fair terms, encountered me with a scrutinizing glance, and inquired where I could have been the entire day.

My answer to his rude interrogations

was

CHAP. VII. 1808.

was in the angrieſt tone I could aſſume. I poured forth a bitter invective againſt his country and his countrymen, and announced my determination to quit Nyborg with all poſſible diſpatch, leſt I ſhould incur a repetition of the ſcandalous treatment I had experienced that morning. This fierceneſs of demeanour on my ſide produced the very oppoſite manifeſtation on the part of my hoſt. He ſmoothed his front on the inſtant, and warmly invited me to ſup with himſelf and his wife in their private room. But I declined the proffered civility, ſaying that I was, juſt then, in no humour for company; and requeſting that my ſupper might be ſent to me in my own apartment. He followed me, however, to my room, entreating me to tell him what had occurred to excite my diſpleaſure; and, in particular, what he himſelf had done

to

to offend me. Now the fact was, I had put on all this ſhow of reſentment for the mere purpoſe of eſcaping the ſociety of the Jew above mentioned, of whom, I confeſs, I was much afraid. He had ſupped frequently with the landlord and myſelf, and I perceived that he eyed me with the ſtrongeſt ſuſpicion, while he kept teaſing me with queſtions with the ill-diſguiſed view of extracting ſomething from me that might afford him an opportunity of denouncing me to the police. So, after aſſuring my hoſt that I had no cauſe to be ill-pleaſed with him perſonally, I related to him what had happened to me during the day, ending, of courſe, with my honourable diſmiſſal by the Colonel. He now redoubled his efforts to pacify me, and begged again and again that I would favour him and his wife with my

Chap. VII. 1808.

my company for that evening; there ſhould be no one there, he ſaid, but themſelves, not even the Jew; and he would endeavour to make me forget my ill-uſage and chagrin by a good ſupper and a bottle of his beſt wine.

Having thus gained my object without betraying myſelf, or even creating ſuſpicion by mentioning my diſlike to the Jew's ſociety, I pretended to be ſoftened, accepted the kind invitation, ate a hearty ſupper, of which, indeed, I ſtood much in want, and ſpent a very agreeable evening.

On my way from my room I paſſed the bottom of the ſtaircaſe which the Marquis and ſome of his officers were at the time aſcending: he leaned over the baniſters, and, in a half-whiſper, and broken Engliſh, ſaid, "Come to me—morrow morning—

ing—eight o'clock." I bowed aſſent and paſſed on. I was punctual to the time, and was received with the utmoſt kindneſs. His Excellency ſaid that he had fully weighed my important communication, and after conſulting with ſome of his officers in whom he placed unreſerved confidence, had finally determined to accept the propoſal of the Engliſh Government, and would immediately proceed to take his meaſures, which, of courſe, required the greateſt circumſpection. Moſt fortunately, he had ſometime before written to Bernadotte, propoſing that he ſhould come to Nyborg and review the Spaniſh troops; to which Bernadotte had partly conſented, but without fixing the time. His Excellency determined to take advantage of this circumſtance; and, under pretence of a general review and inſpection, to collect

as

as many of his troops as he could at head-quarters. He expreſſed his ſorrow that it was not in his power to place me out of danger, adviſed me not to delay my departure, leſt I ſhould excite ſuſpicion by my long ſojourn at his hotel; thanked me cordially for the valuable ſervice I had rendered him at ſuch imminent riſk, and aſſured me, that if it ſhould pleaſe God to reſtore him to his country, he would on all occaſions be ready to bear his cordial teſtimony to the admirable manner in which I had executed my commiſſion. After this aſſurance he again expreſſed his ſtrong anxiety for my perſonal ſafety, and in the kindeſt and moſt condeſcending manner bade me farewell.

Thus ended my laſt interview with this excellent and patriotic nobleman. I left him impreſſed with an exalted idea

idea of his virtuous and dignified character, and with feelings of intense interest for the success of the undertaking to which he was now committed; an undertaking so hazardous to himself, so pregnant with momentous consequences to his country and the cause of Europe.

CHAPTER VIII.

Alarms and difficulties encountered in the Return to Hamburg. Small apparent chance of eſcaping thence to England. Welcome tidings of the Evaſion of La Romana and the greater part of the Troops under his command.

CHAP. VIII.

1808.

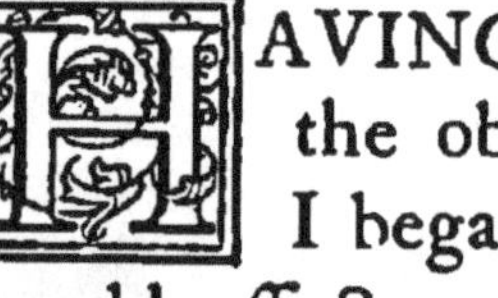

HAVING now accompliſhed the object of my miſſion, I began to conſider how I ſhould effect my return, which, indeed, ſeemed beſet with difficulties not leſs formidable than thoſe which had attended my journey hither.

I told my landlord that finding it impracticable

impracticable to reach Copenhagen, as was my original intention, and having got a few orders from the Marquis, I ſhould, without loſs of time, ſet out on my return to Hamburg. He expreſſed regret at loſing me ſo ſoon, and begged I would have the goodneſs to take an order from him for the inn-keeper at Aſſens, his ſtock of rum and brandy being almoſt exhauſted.

The following morning I took leave of my hoſt and proceeded, without interruption, to Aſſens, where my paſſport had formerly been examined and marked. But I was doomed to meet with a very ſerious impediment on this occaſion, and one which might,—had my ſelf-poſſeſſion failed,—have put an effectual ſtop to my further progreſs. On entering the hotel, or coffee-houſe, I took notice of a group of men who were buſy

CHAP. VIII. 1808.

bufy over their bottle, and obferved among them one of particularly ferocious afpect, who rofe almoft immediately, and, with the authoritative air of a man in office, demanded my paffport. It was produced accordingly, when cafting his eye over it in a manner which convinced me he could not read it, he declared it "not good." I was much provoked at his infolent manner, and could not refrain from ufing angry words towards himfelf and his affociates, which, however, he bore with perfect indifference. I found my way to a private room, where my luggage had been left, but hither he followed me and infifted on infpecting my portmanteau. I offered no refiftance, and he proceeded to unfold every article it contained. Even my dreffing cafe underwent a ftrict examination; and when he difcovered my fhavingſhaving-bruſh rolled up in a piece of paper, he ſeized on the poor ſcrap with the greateſt avidity. Alas! nothing but diſappointment awaited him,—it was part of a letter, of no conſequence whatſoever, and written in German; for I had taken particular care that there ſhould be nothing Engliſh about me to create ſuſpicion. Foiled in this, he turned his thoughts another way; and when I went down to diſcharge my chaiſe, he inſiſted on ſeeing in what coin I was going to pay the poſtilion. I was determined that I would not ſubmit to this piece of inſolence, and poſitively refuſed to pay the man a ſhilling while he looked on. The poor poſtilion ſtood trembling all the while, and was only too happy to have an excuſe for driving away, fearing, doubtleſs, that he might be called to account for having brought

a

a ſuſpicious perſon into the town; ſo he actually left Aſſens without receiving his fare. The man in authority then withdrew, taking my paſſport with him. My troubles were not yet at an end, for the landlord of the hotel, who had been hitherto a ſilent ſpectator, now came forward and began to make an apology for not being able to accommodate me; but I cut him ſhort by obſerving that it was a matter of no conſequence; that I had indeed intended to give him a conſiderable order which I had received from the keeper of the principal hotel at Nyborg, for rum and brandy, but that I would now reſerve it for ſome one elſe. The effect was electrical, the change from ſmothered inſolence to open ſervility was inſtantaneous. Every thing was at my command,—rather than diſappoint any gentleman coming

ing from that houſe (at Nyborg), and bringing ſuch recommendations as I had brought, he would turn all his other cuſtomers out of doors. This ſudden alteration had, of courſe, the effect of reconciling me; and, as nothing was to be gained by leaving his houſe, I agreed to ſtay there that night, and delivered to him the order I had received for the foreign ſpirits.

My paſſport was returned to me in about two hours by the ſame official perſonage who had taken it, and who now, with many apologies for the trouble I had been put to, informed me that it was perfectly good.

I left Aſſens the following morning, after giving money to my hoſt to ſatisfy the demands of my timorous poſtilion, and proceeded on my journey homewards.

I choſe the ſame route I had before

before taken, paſſing through Kiel to Lübeck, and thence to Hamburg, without any ſerious interruption. Here I took lodgings in one of the ſuburbs, that I might avoid the interrogatories at the gates of the town; and I embraced the opportunity offered me of writing to Mr. McKenzie, at Heligoland, to report the ſucceſsful accompliſhment of my miſſion, and to requeſt that inſtructions might be ſent to the commanders of the Britiſh fleet in the Baltic, to hold themſelves in readineſs to communicate with the Spaniſh General.

My chief ſolicitude now was as to the means of effecting my own eſcape, the obſtacles to which appeared inſurmountable. I endeavoured to get off by Cuxhaven, but found this impracticable. My thoughts then reverted to my old friend

friend the smuggler, who had so admirably managed my landing on the Continent; accordingly I set off for Bremen, and paid him a visit at his house in the country. It would be difficult to exaggerate the surprise and alarm which he manifested on beholding me. Without giving me time to speak, he cried out, "For God's sake, begone! I know what you want—I absolutely can do nothing for you. Do not bring ruin upon me by staying under my roof." On coming to an explanation, I found that he had fallen under suspicion after my departure, and that his house had been most strictly searched. Unwilling, therefore, again to compromise his safety, I returned immediately to Brèmen, and from Bremen to my old lodgings in the vicinity of Hamburg.

And here I received the happy tidings

Chap. VIII. 1808.

tidings of the Marquis de la Romana's eſcape with the greater part of his army. I ſhould vainly attempt to deſcribe my feelings on this occaſion. To know that, through my humble inſtrumentality, upwards of ten thouſand men had been reſcued from exile and reſtored to their country, their homes, and the cauſe of Europe, overpowered me with joy; and my gratitude to God, who had enabled me to perform this great ſervice, and miraculouſly preſerved me through all the dangers attendant upon ſo ſerious an undertaking, was without bounds. But a few days after, I had the mortification of ſeeing ſome of the poor Spaniards, who had been unable to get off, brought priſoners into Hamburg. One day, two Spaniſh officers entered the ſhop of my landlord, who was a ſaddler, to diſpoſe of ſome of the trappings

trappings of their horfes. I was in the fhop at the time, and addreffed fome queftions to them in French. The fury they difplayed on the inftant was terrific, and I verily believe, that on the mere prefumption of my being a Frenchman, I fhould have fuffered perfonal maltreatment at their hands, had I not now, in abfolute fear of my life, avowed myfelf an Englifhman. I now ran almoft equal rifk from their extravagant demonftrations of affection, for they caught me in their arms, kiffed me, called me a thoufand times the *bueno Ingles*, and almoft fmothered me in their embraces. When they had a little recovered from their tranfport, and I from its confequences, we entered into converfation, as well as we could, in Italian, and I learned from them fome particulars attending La Romana's efcape from Nyborg. I

endeavoured

endeavoured to gather their opinion as to the feelings which the Spaniards generally entertained towards Bonaparte. I pretended to ſhow the utter hopeleſſneſs of any attempt on the part of Spain to ſhake off the French yoke. "Look," ſaid I, "at the ſtate of Europe, proſtrate at the feet of the Corſican: his power acknowledged from Paris to Moſcow: from the German Ocean to Naples and Sicily: from Stockholm and Copenhagen to Liſbon and Cadiz. It is vain attempting to reſiſt his aſcendency—you muſt obey—*biſogna ubbidire.*"

They had liſtened ſo far with impatience, but they could bear it no longer, and they ejaculated with vehemence, "*Ubbidire! Morire prima.*"

Having thus elicited the ſpirit of theſe two Spaniards, and received an impreſſion that the people of the country generally were of the ſame mind

CHAP. VIII.

1808.

mind, I warmly expreſſed the pleaſure I felt at witneſſing their enthuſiaſm, and confeſſed that I looked to Spain with ſome hope as the field where the final ſtruggle for the liberty of Europe would be decided. They declared their confidence in the ſpirit of their countrymen. "Give them but arms and leaders," ſaid they, "and they will ſhed the laſt drop of their blood to maintain their country's independence."

After ſome more converſation of the ſame kind, we bade each other farewell, with aſſurances on both ſides of eſteem and friendſhip, and prayers for the ſucceſs of the good cauſe.

Chapter

Chapter IX.

Of the manner in which La Romana effected the withdrawal of his Troops —Notice of his subsequent history.

Chap. IX.

1808.

N first receiving the intelligence of the Spanish army having got off, I communicated it to Mr. McKenzie, through the usual channel, viz. Cuxhaven, and desired that when the announcement of the great fact appeared in the English papers, it should be stated that the individual, who had opened the communication with La Romana on the part of the British Government,

Government, had happily returned in ſafety to England. This, I thought, might tend in ſome degree to lull the vigilance of the French emiſſaries on the Continent,—a point of vital importance to me, ſince, as matters ſtood, I found it perfectly impoſſible, notwithſtanding my knowledge of the country and its language, to effect my eſcape.

It will not be improper in this place briefly to relate the manner in which La Romana managed his delicate undertaking, and ſome of the circumſtances attendant on the embarkation of his army.

He began, as I before mentioned, to collect as many of his troops as poſſible at Nyborg, and whilſt employed in this way he wrote again to Bernadotte, urging him to come thither and review the army at his earlieſt convenience. In conſequence of

CHAP. IX.
1808.

of this requeſt, Bernadotte was on the point of ſetting out for Nyborg with only a few attendants, when the Spaniſh Colonel mentioned in a former part of this narrative, (who was living in the vicinity of Hamburg for his health,) interpoſed with his advice that he ſhould take a detachment of troops with him, as he (the Colonel) ſtrongly ſuſpected treachery. Upon this, Bernadotte haſtily collected about 3,000 men, and marched for Nyborg with all poſſible expedition. La Romana was informed of his being on the way, and determined at once to embark with that portion of his army which he had got together, conſiſting of about 10,000 men. Having prepared all his meaſures, he invited the civic officers of Nyborg and the principal inhabitants, together with his own officers, to a grand entertaiment tainment. After the *déjeûner*, the troops were ordered to go through their manœuvres for the gratification of the company, and, according to inſtructions, the officers proceeded to ſurround the hotel. The Marquis then ſtood up, and addreſſing his gueſts, aſſured them all of their perſonal ſafety, but added, that peculiar circumſtances rendered it imperative on him to put them under a temporary arreſt. At the laſt mentioned word, two French officers who were of the company, ſtarted up and laid their hands on their ſwords, ejaculating, in wonder and indignation, "Arreſt!" "Gentlemen," continued the Marquis, "reſiſtance is perfectly uſeleſs;" upon which the door opened, and in ruſhed a party of grenadiers, with fixed bayonets. The Frenchmen, ſeeing the folly of oppoſition, delivered their ſwords. The

Chap. IX.
1808.

The Spaniards immediately marched down to the harbour and preſſed into their ſervice every boat and bark which could aſſiſt them in reaching the Engliſh fleet. On a ſignal being given, the Engliſh boats put in to their aſſiſtance, and a ſcene of activity and buſtle enſued ſuch as the inhabitants of Nyborg had never witneſſed before. When the whole of the Spaniards had embarked, except about 300 men who were covering the embarkation, Bernadotte arrived with his army, and found, to his confuſion, that his priſoner, as he well might have deemed him, had eluded his vigilance, and was already beyond his reach.

The handful of Spaniards who remained on land, putting themſelves in an attitude of defence, ſhowed a determination to ſell their lives as dearly as poſſible, but the

Colonel

Chap. IX.

1808.

Colonel who commanded them, riding to their front and pointing out to them, in a few words, the hopelessness of any resistance to a force so much superior to their own, desired them to lay down their arms. They reluctantly complied. He then dismounted, and, taking the pistols from his holster, shot his charger, ejaculating, "But as for thee, they shall never mount thee; and me," he continued, putting a pistol to his head, "they shall never disarm." Thus, by his own hand, fell this high-minded Spaniard—a sacrifice, in the prime of life, to an overstrained sentiment of chivalrous honour, which, though we are forced to condemn it, we find it difficult not to admire.

Bernadotte returned to Hamburg with his prisoners to brood over his disappointment. La Romana and his army

army ſailed for England, and ſubſequently for Spain, where they did good ſervice in the field. Romana's preſence in Spain was ſpecially important, on account of his intimate knowledge of the country, of its reſources, and of the ſpirit of the people. He powerfully aided the common cauſe by inſpiring the nation with confidence in their Engliſh allies, aſſiſting theſe with his valuable advice, and zealouſly co-operating with them in all their operations. He was beloved by the army and the people—beloved by all who had the good of Spain at heart—for his pure and diſintereſted patriotiſm and for his kind and conciliatory manners. He was hated with equal ſincerity by all who aimed at enriching themſelves through the ruin of their country, on account of his inflexible probity and the ceaſeleſs

ceaſeleſs vigilance by which he detected their moſt ſecret plots and cabals.

Such was the man who, with ten thouſand of the beſt troops of Spain, was, through my humble inſtrumentality, reſtored to his country in the very criſis of her fortunes, to act a vigorous part in the memorable ſtruggle againſt her oppreſſors. To the value of his ſervices in that great conflict we have the higheſt teſtimony of his friend and brother in arms—the Duke of Wellington, who, in deſpatches written ſoon after La Romana's death (in 1811), ſays: "His talents, his virtues, and his patriotiſm were well known to His Majeſty's Government, and I ſhall always acknowledge with gratitude the aſſiſtance I have received from him, as well by his operations as by his counſel. In him the Spaniſh army

Chap. IX.
1808.

army have loſt their brighteſt ornament, his country their moſt upright patriot, and the world the moſt ſtrenuous and zealous defender of the cauſe in which we are engaged."

The following ſhort memoir appeared in the *Liſbon Gazette*:—

"Senhor Don Pedro Caro y Sureda, Marquis of Romana, Grandee of Spain, Knight of the Grand Croſs of the Royal Order of Charles III, Captain-General of the armies of his Catholic Majeſty, was born at Palma, the capital of the Iſland of Majorça. After an education ſuitable to his high birth, during which he made rapid progreſs in Latin, Greek, and Hebrew, emulous of his father's glory, who terminated his life moſt honourably in the expedition againſt Algiers in 1775, he commenced his military career in the Marine Guards in in the Royal fleet, where he continued till the revolutionary war with France; at which period, being captain of a frigate, he entered with the rank of colonel into the army of Navarre, under the orders of his uncle, Lieutenant-General Don Ventura Caro, and afterwards into that of Catalonia, in which, by his valour and ſignal ſervices, he worthily obtained ſucceſſive poſts, and arrived at the rank of Lieutenant-General. In 1801 he was appointed Captain-General of Catalonia and Preſident of its Royal Audience, in which employment he had occaſion to diſplay his great abilities and political knowledge. He was afterwards named General of the Engineers and Counſellor of War. The inſidious views of the Tyrant of Europe induced him to ſeparate from Spain the greater part of her beſt troops, in the

Chap. IX.

1808.

the command of whom Romana conducted himſelf with all the propriety and delicacy he was ſo noted for. In the midſt of the ſnows of the North, he was informed by a confidential agent* of the Government, not without the moſt imminent danger, of the ſtate of his beloved country. He vowed to ſuccour it with his troops, to accompliſh which he overcame a thouſand difficulties and dangers. In the command of the army of the North he executed moſt ſkilful retreats and movements, ſuſpending and fruſtrating the projects of the enemy, whoſe forces were always ſuperior. A ſhort time after he was called to the Central Junta, where he preſented himſelf, not as a victorious General,

* The Rev. J. Robertſon.

General, but as the moſt modeſt Repreſentative, manifeſting all the force of his character in the vote that he gave, in the month of October, 1809, upon the neceſſity of forming a Council of Regency. On the 24th of January following, finding the ſupreme government diſperſed by the invaſion of Andaluſia by the French, he returned to take the command of the army of Eſtramadura, where his preſence was of ſuch importance, that to it, in a great meaſure, was owing the enthuſiaſm manifeſted at Badajos and throughout the province. The endeavours the enemy made from that time, and the dexterity with which Romana knew to oppoſe them and defeat their plans, we well know, until Eſtramadura being free, and Maſſena advancing upon the lines of Torres Vedras, he haſtened with two

Chap. IX.
1808.

two diviſions of his army to the aſſiſtance of the Allies. On his way, and in the city of Liſbon, he received many proofs of eſtimation. Afterwards he fought conſtantly at the ſide of his illuſtrious friend, Lord Wellington, the worthy appreciator of his merits and virtues, whoſe teſtimony alone would be ſufficient to prove the great loſs which Spain and the common cauſe of the Allies have ſuffered by his death, were we even without proofs of the public enthuſiaſm which his name and fame inſpired in all parts.

"Romana died, after a ſhort illneſs, at Cartaxo, the head-quarters of Lord Wellington, the 23rd of January, 1811, in the 49th year of his age.

Chapter

CHAPTER X.

Perſonal Narrative reſumed. Eſcape to England immediately, or by a direct route, found impracticable. Circuitous journey through Central and Southern Germany. Erfurth the Head-quarters of the French Emperor. Retroſpective Notice of a tranſaction which had brought the Author into contact with Napoleon when Firſt Conſul. Ratiſbon and Lintz. Sojourn there. Munich. Intelligence of the French reverſes in Spain circulated through Bavaria by the Author's agency. Important diſcovery of his proceedings. Haſty return to Lintz.

After

Chap. X.

1808.

FTER my unſucceſsful attempts to elude the vigilance of the enemy and to eſcape to England, I turned my thoughts towards my old abode in Ratiſbon; propoſing to myſelf to paſs ſome time in the ſouth of Germany, and there to await a favourable opportunity of returning to my native country. I reſolved to take Erfurth in my route, and gratify my curioſity by ſeeing once more the Arbiter of the Continental Nations, who was then holding his celebrated conference with the Emperor Alexander. Though I had been the agent in counteracting one of his keeneſt ſtrokes of policy, yet I felt that no compunction, on that ſcore, would ſtir within me at his preſence, nor was I afraid of his penetrating eye. I had ſeen him ſome years before,

before, ere he had aſſumed the Imperial purple, and had even received from him what I regarded as a great, though it was not a perſonal, favour. During the peace of Amiens I had viſited Paris; and, finding that in the ſweeping confiſcation of monaſtic property, which was one of the prominent features of that ſhort-lived truce, the Scotch Seminary at Ratiſbon, in which I had been educated, was to ſhare the general doom, I haſtily drew up and preſented to the Firſt Conſul a memorial, calling his attention to the peculiar ſituation of that eſtabliſhment, which, though under the ſuperintendence of the abbot and monks of the Scotch Benedictine Abbey, and located within the walls of that ancient houſe of religion, was, nevertheleſs, a ſeparate and diſtinct foundation, intended only for the education of of Scottiſh youth, without reference to their ulterior deſtination; conſequently, it was neither an eccleſiaſtical nor a monaſtic inſtitution. Bonaparte acknowledged the juſtice of the plea; and orders were iſſued to exempt the Scotch Seminary from the confiſcation. Need I ſuggeſt that, had I now chanced to attract his notice, and had he diſcovered that the humble ſuppliant for his favour on one occaſion had been the zealous and ſucceſsful agent of his implacable enemies on another, I ſhould have had little mercy to expect at his hands? But, as I ſaid above, I had a ſtrong deſire to viſit Erfurth, and thither I went, taking up my abode in the Scotch monaſtery there, which was a branch of that in Ratiſbon, and under the ſame abbot.* After a

* The Seminary remains to this day, and is conducted

a short sojourn with my old colleagues, the brothers Hamilton, then professors of that University, I left for Ratisbon; and on my way visited the field of the celebrated battle of Jena, which only three years before had proved so fatal to the Prussian Monarchy. It was my fate that I, peaceful as my profession was, should, like too many a brave soldier, have reason to remember that field; for, in passing over some very uneven ground, I accidentally fell, and cut my knee severely. I tried to console myself

conducted on the same principles, and in the same manner as it had been previously to the period here spoken of, though the Monastery was handed over to the Archbishop of Mayence, as part of the indemnity granted to him for the loss of his Electoral territory on the Rhine. The Monastery likewise remains, though the number of its inmates is reduced; but being now re-established by the King of Bavaria, it is expected to flourish again. Ed.

Chap. X.

1808.

myſelf for my miſhap by the thought that I ſhould always be able to boaſt of having fallen and bled on the field of Jena.

I reached Ratiſbon in ſafety, but remained there only a few weeks, proceeding thence to Lintz, which I made my head-quarters for the winter. Here I had the ſociety of my old friend and colleague, Mr. Alexander Horn; and poſſeſſed the advantage of conſtant communication with London. On receiving, while ſtill at Lintz, the account of one of the moſt ſignal victories gained by Lord Wellington over the French in Spain, I determined on ſpreading the news as much as poſſible; and for that purpoſe tranſlated the Duke's diſpatches into German, and had them printed for diſtribution. The more fully to effect my purpoſe of giving a wide publicity to the diſaſters of the

the French army in the Peninſula, I took a ſecret journey to Munich, where I had an old friend, who, though admitted to the inner circle of the Court, was, I knew, for certain cogent reaſons, by no means well affected to the French party in that capital. To him I made my object known, and with his connivance I ſallied out during the darkneſs of the evening, and in various parts of the city dropped a number of the printed documents which I had brought with me. I was, of courſe, not inſenſible to the danger of the enterpriſe, and was, therefore, not much ſurpriſed when, ſhortly after reaching my friend's houſe, he returned from a viſit to the palace, and informed me that ſome of the papers had already found their way thither, and were creating the greateſt excitement. He adviſed me to depart

part at once, and repaſs the frontiers of Bavaria with all poſſible diſpatch. The advice of a friend ſo clear-ſighted and judicious was not to be deſpiſed, and I therefore followed it to the letter; urging my poſtilions, by a liberal diſtribution of gold, to put the mettle of their cattle to the proof, until I found myſelf once more in the territories of Auſtria. How needful all my ſpeed had been, I was ſoon convinced by a letter I received from my kind monitor, informing me that I had ſcarcely left Munich when orders were iſſued to the police to ſhut the gates, and inſtitute the ſtricteſt poſſible ſearch for the incendiary who had dared to circulate ſuch intelligence in the ſtronghold of French influence in Germany. And on the preſumption that, after ſcattering his hand-bills, he might have betaken himſelf to flight, light troops

Chap. X. 1808.

troops were dispatched in every direction, with orders to bring in the suspected criminal, dead or alive. I need not say how grateful I felt for my providential deliverance from so great a danger; for there can be little doubt that my arrest would have led to the discovery, not only of the author and disseminator of the noxious hand-bills, but of the agent who had managed the escape of la Romana; and I should, of course, have been delivered over to the tender mercies of Bonaparte.

Chapter XI.

Further removal from Lintz to Vienna and Dreſden. Imminent peril encountered in the latter city. Flight and purſuit through Berlin and Hamburg to the coaſt. Safe Arrival in England. Backward glance on the incidents of the Miſſion. Concluſion.

Chap. XI.

1809.

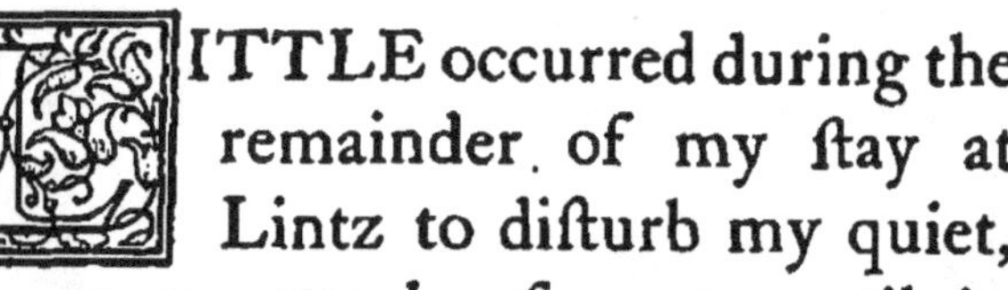

LITTLE occurred during the remainder of my ſtay at Lintz to diſturb my quiet, except an attack of gout, until in the ſpring of 1809 the French ſwept through Germany, driving the Auſtrian army, under the Archduke Charles, before them; and, though laſt,

Chap. XI. 1809.

laſt, not leaſt, in my own eſtimation, I too, was forced to quit my quiet domicile, gout and all, and flee for ſafety. Arrived in Vienna, I ſoon found that even there I ſhould not long be ſafe; and accordingly made immediate arrangements for leaving that capital. The north of Germany was at that time comparatively quiet; for, though the French had puſhed forward corps into Saxony, to keep the Auſtrians in check in that quarter, yet the great theatre of war to which the eyes of Europe were directed, lay in the hereditary dominions of the Emperor. Impreſſed with an opinion that my eſcape through the north would be eaſier, now that the ſouth abſorbed the attention of the conflicting nations, I at once adopted the reſolution of attempting my retreat from the Continent. I quitted Vienna and poſted through Bohemia, without

Chap. XI.

1809.

without a paſſport, towards Dreſden. Within ſome miles of the latter place I met an Auſtrian general officer, attended by a ſingle trooper. To him I addreſſed a brief inquiry. I told him I was deſirous of entering Dreſden, but had no paſſport; and wiſhed to know whether the city was ſtill in the occupation of the Auſtrians under Marſhal Keenmayer. His replies were equally brief; and, ſo far, ſatisfactory. "I am Marſhal Keenmayer. The army under my command has evacuated Dreſden, and is encamped near the town. The French army is encamped on the oppoſite ſide, and has not, as yet, taken poſſeſſion of it;—if you make haſte you may reach it in ſafety. Good morning." I loſt no time, and entered the city without a queſtion being aſked. Within two hours the place was occupied by the French; and

and in a ſhort ſpace I had the honour of a viſit, at my hotel, from two officers of the police, kindly to inquire my name and occupation. I gave my aſſumed name, Adam Rorauer, and announced myſelf as a teacher of languages. They ſeemed ſatisfied with my anſwer and left me. In about two or three hours they returned and inquired whether I had a paſſport. "No." "You have given us a wrong name—yours is James Robertſon—you are a native of Scotland." Imagine, reader, if you can, the ſtartling effect of this announcement on my nerves. I was thunderſtruck. But having, in a manner, become familiar with ſuch incidents, I, fortunately, recovered my preſence of mind without attracting the particular attention of the queriſts, and replied, with aſſumed compoſure—"Well, what then? I am ſtill a teacher

Chap. XI.
1809.

teacher of languages." "But, ſir," they anſwered, "you cannot ſtop here." "I am content—give me a paſſport." "Sir, you came without a paſſport, and therefore you cannot have one from hence." "Then let me go without one." "That is equally impoſſible," was the reply. I could only exclaim againſt this inconſiſtency; and they left me, for further inſtructions, as I preſumed, promiſing another viſit.

The dilemma was ſerious, and prompt deciſion was neceſſary to extricate me from my difficulties. How my name had been diſcovered, I could not even ſurmiſe, nor have I ſince aſcertained; but I felt fully perſuaded that little time would ſuffice for ſuch further diſcoveries as would place my life in danger.

It was my happineſs to have been ſaved at Munich by one friend who

who had formerly belonged to the ſame religious community as myſelf; and I firmly believe that, upon the preſent trying occaſion, I owed my ſafety to another. The worthy eccleſiaſtic of whom I ſpeak, held the office of chaplain in a family of the higheſt diſtinction, then reſident in the neighbourhood of Dreſden. While gratefully acknowledging the important ſervice which he rendered me, I rejoice to record the good fortune which ſubſequently befell him in being appointed preceptor to the Crown Prince of Bavaria, and a canon of the Cathedral of Ratiſbon. To him I communicated my difficulties, entreating the exerciſe of his local knowledge and influence to procure me a paſſport for Berlin. I, or rather he, was ſucceſsful. I obtained the neceſſary document, and left immediately for the Pruſſian capital,

Chap. XI.

1809.

capital, with a firm determination not to cry halt, until I ſhould have ſhaken the duſt of Continental ſoil from my feet. I kept to my reſolution; and poſting, without the leaſt regard to expenſe, to Berlin—from Berlin to Hamburg, from Hamburg, by the ſhorteſt route, to the coaſt—had the good fortune to reach Cuxhaven in ſafety.

I was now among friends, who ſoon conveyed me to Heligoland; and I reached Harwich by the packet in due courſe.

Some time after my arrival in London, I received information from a friend in Hamburg, who was in the confidence of our Government, that exactly what I had expected had come to paſs. Almoſt immediately after my departure from Dreſden, the police, or the French, had diſcovered who I was; I had been tracked and purſued by huſſars through Berlin and Hamburg; but, though always cloſe at my heels, by ſome chance, inexplicable alike to them and to my friend, before reaching the coaſt they had loſt all traces of me.

The only way in which I could account for my eſcape was this:—I have mentioned that I did not ſpare expenſe; and, I may add, I paid the poſtilions extravagantly. My fame, of courſe, kept pace with my progreſs; and, near the end of my journey, my poſtilions wiſhing to make the moſt of their good cuſtomer, ſuggeſted that, as the horſes (I travelled with four) were in excellent condition, the ſtages rather ſhort, and I in ſuch evident haſte, they would take me on a ſecond ſtage without ſtopping. To this I aſſented. When we arrived near the end of the firſt ſtage, the poſtilions, being

Chap. XI.

1809.

being afraid of the poſt-maſter, who would probably not have permitted them to proceed without changing horſes, took a circuitous route to avoid the village. In the meantime, as I conjecture, my purſuers came up; but finding, upon inquiry at the village, that I had not paſſed through, probably ſuſpected that I had followed ſome ſide-road, to baffle purſuit; and themſelves tried every route but the right one.

Such is the incident to which alone I could attribute my providential eſcape from the laſt, and perhaps the moſt ſerious, of all the varied riſks I had run in the courſe of my adventurous undertaking.

I was now beyond the reach of my enemies, and had full time calmly to reflect on the continual danger to which I had been expoſed from my firſt leaving England until my landing

ing again at Harwich—a period of thirteen months. The earlier ſtages of my expedition, including my landing at Bremen, my progreſs to the Marquis de la Romana's head-quarters—my ſtay at Nyborg and my return to Hamburg, appeared at the time the moſt perilous, becauſe then the danger, ſtaring me as it were in the face, I felt that at any moment I might loſe my preſence of mind, and *that* would at once have been fatal to me; yet now, as I look back on the paſt, it ſeems to me that I was even in greater jeopardy whilſt repoſing quietly during the winter at Lintz. For, had I been diſcovered there by any of the French ſpies, beyond all doubt Bonaparte would have demanded that I ſhould be delivered up to him; and it is equally certain that, before the open rupture between the two powers, Auſtria would, in ſuch

Chap. XI.

1809.

ſuch a contingency, have complied with the requeſt. Nay, it is more than probable that the Auſtrians, who were doing all in their power to blind Bonaparte to their real deſigns, would have delivered me up of their own accord, had they found out who I was, and upon what buſineſs I had been employed. But the cloſing act of the eventful hiſtory, embracing my haſty retreat from Lintz to Vienna, and thence to Dreſden, the diſcovery there of my name and country, my flight and purſuit almoſt to the water's edge, was the moſt truly perilous of all; for what had been wanting to the danger of the firſt two periods had been realized in the laſt. I had been diſcovered, and diſcovery, had I been taken, would have proved the brief precurſor of death.

In the calmneſs of perfect ſecurity in

in which I now found myſelf, the various feelings by which I had been ſo long agitated frequently came back upon my mind with little leſs than their original force. The hope at ſtarting; the fear inſpired by dangers encountered at the outſet; the inceſſant dread of diſcovery at a time when diſcovery would have involved the failure of my miſſion, as well as the extremity of peril to myſelf; the thrilling ſuſpenſe I endured during my hazardous conferences with La Romana; the cruel diſappointment I experienced when baffled in my attempt to get on board one of the Engliſh ſhips of war; the delight with which I firſt heard of the eſcape of La Romana and his troops; the ever-recurring alarms which beſet me during the long period of my baniſhment, and the intenſe anxiety which accompanied every ſtep

step of my homeward journey to England,—all were reproduced in turn, only to be replaced by the deep sense of joy at my deliverance, and triumph in the accomplishment of the great object to which my energies had been devoted. With these emotions—let me confess it—was mingled no small degree of pride at having succeeded in so momentous and difficult an undertaking, when others, apparently far better qualified for the attempt by their previous pursuits and habits of life, had engaged in it and failed.

Every fresh report of advantages gained by the British or Spanish armies, and particularly by the army under La Romana; every praise bestowed upon him personally; every comment on his usefulness and on the importance of his counsel, and of his influence to the success of the great

great cauſe, awakened in me feelings of ſelf-gratulation. But high above all predominated a ſentiment of heartfelt gratitude to God, who had enabled me to be the ſucceſsful inſtrument in accompliſhing ſo much good, and in the midſt of innumerable dangers had preſerved my life and permitted me to witneſs the happy conſequences of my exertions.

APPENDIX.

Memoir of the Marquis de La Romana.

EXTRACTED FROM THE "BIOGRAPHIE UNIVERSELLE."

EDRO Caro y Sureda, Marquis de la Romana, was born on the 3rd of October, 1761, at Palma, the capital of the Island of Majorca. His father was a general officer, who, while commanding the Spanish vanguard in the expedition against Algiers in 1775, fell in action at the head of the Almanza regiment of dragoons. The young La Romana was sent to France in 1771, and received a very careful education in the College of the Oratory at Lyons. He continued his studies at the University of Salamanca and the Seminary of Nobles, at Madrid, where he made rapid progress in science and even in the arts.

He

He had been appointed a marine guard in 1775, but it was not till 1778 that he entered on the difcharge of his functions, repairing for that purpofe to the academy of his corps eftablifhed at Carthagena. His good conduct and the talents which he difplayed raifed him to the rank of an officer in 1779, and a fhort time afterwards General Don Véntura Moreno chofe him for his adjutant. In 1782 he ferved with diftinction in the gunboats and floating batteries at the fiege of Gibraltar. At the peace of 1783 he retired to Valencia, where he devoted his leifure to the cultivation of literature, and more particularly to the ftudy of languages. He at this time dedicated the greater part of his income to the collection of a valuable library and the encouragement of Spanifh artifts applying themfelves to fculpture and to painting. In 1784 he left his home to vifit foreign countries, with the view of increafing his ftores of knowledge, and made fome confiderable ftay at Vienna and Berlin, where he found every facility to improve his acquaintance with the art of war. On his return from his travels he went to fea under the command of Gravina, and in 1790 was appointed captain of a frigate. When the war broke out between Spain and France, La Romana paffed over to the land fervice.

He

He was employed at firſt under the orders of his uncle, Don Ventura Caro, general-in-chief of the army of Guipuſcoa, who, knowing his bravery and his adventurous character, gave him the command of a corps of chaſſeurs, conſiſting of about 2,000 men. This command La Romana continued to hold throughout the campaign of 1793, and for the greater part of 1794. On the 30th of April, 1793, he contributed to the taking of the camp of Sare, which the Spaniards abandoned after having plundered and burnt it; and on the 6th of June following, he diſtinguiſhed himſelf in the action at Château-Pignon, where the general-in-chief of the French army, La Genetière, was beaten and made priſoner. Müller, who ſucceeded La Genetière, having attacked the line of the Spaniſh poſts in the valley of Bäigorri, and made himſelf maſter of the village of Aldudes, evinced his intention of occupying the valleys of Baſtan and Roncesvalles, and menacing Pampeluna. To effect a diverſion, Caro brought together 10,000 or 12,000 men on the Bidaſſoa, and dividing them into four columns, put them ſimultaneouſly into motion on the 23rd of June, 1794. La Romana, who commanded the ſecond column, ſetting out from Biriaton, directed his march on Mont Diamant and

Mont

Mont Vert, and there established himself, driving back the French. General Escalante was equally successful at the head of the first column, but the other two, having been less fortunate, were obliged to fall back on the troops of Escalante and La Romana, to whom they communicated their own disorder; the discomfiture then became general, and the Spaniards were constrained to recross the Bidassoa. After his defeat at the camp of St. Martial and the loss of Fontarabia, on the 1st of August, 1794, General Caro was recalled, and his place was supplied by the Count de Colomera. La Romana being now transferred to the army of Catalonia, under the command of the Count de la Union, distinguished himself, we are told, at the battle of Montenegro, on the 18th and 20th of November. The rout of the Spaniards on that occasion was complete; about 10,000 of their soldiers were left on the field of battle, 8,000 were made prisoners, and three generals —La Union himself, the chief in command, being one—were among the slain.* The fort of Figueras, which had been deemed impregnable, was forced to surrender, and the wreck

* Dugommier, the commander-in-chief of the French army, had been killed in the action of the 18th by the bursting of a shell, and was succeeded by Perignon.

wreck of the Spaniſh army was compelled to ſhut itſelf up in Girona. Amidſt the general confuſion, the corps of La Romana was the only one that retired in good order; he covered the retreat, and more than once checked the purſuit of the enemy.

Promoted ſoon after to the rank of major-general, he ſerved under the Marquis de las Amarillas, who had aſſumed the command of the Spaniſh army after the death of La Union, and under Don Joſef de Urrutia, who was ſhortly appointed in his ſtead. The latter general, finding his force inſufficient to relieve the fort of Roſas, which the French were vigorouſly beſieging, endeavoured, by means of a diverſion, to draw away the French to another point. Don Ildefonſo Arias received orders to puſh forward to the banks of the Fluvia, and threaten the French poſitions on that ſide; while La Romana, with 2,000 men, was to make a movement on their left, and endeavour to ſurpriſe their cantonments. The latter only was able to execute the movement preſcribed to him. Setting out from Bezalu, following the road to Figueras and paſſing by Criſpia, he, on the 16th of January, 1795, reached the level of the poſts which he was inſtructed to ſeize, and within 300 paces of the French advanced guard. He immediately took

took measures to carry two of the French cantonments by surprise, but his plan was frustrated by the imprudence of a Spanish corporal, who answered the summons of a sentinel by discharging his musket. The report startled the French, and made them aware of the danger to which they were exposed. The main-guard, alarmed at the sight of the Spaniards, had already thrown down their arms, and were flying in disorder, when succours came up. La Romana then gave orders to his advanced guard to fall back and form in line behind his cavalry. The French, mistaking this movement for a retreat, advanced in their turn, but were vigorously repelled by the Spanish cavalry, and forced to make a rampart of their bayonets. During this charge, the Spanish infantry had re-formed; the cavalry then opened their ranks, and while they bore down rapidly on the flanks of the republicans, the infantry attacked them with such impetuosity, that they could not withstand the shock. La Romana, at this conjuncture, performed prodigies of valour. Placing himself at the head of his cavalry, he charged the right flank of the French, and threw them into disorder. But by this time the troops encamped below Figueras had been put in motion to carry aid

to

to the defeated party. La Romana, who had had two horſes killed under him, receiving timely notice of this movement, gave orders to diſcontinue the purſuit, and reluctantly abandoning the field of battle, retired in good order on Bezalu. He afterwards took part in the ſanguinary engagements of the 28th of March and 5th of May, 1795, in which both parties claimed to have had the advantage. The moſt important event of this campaign was the taking of Roſas, which was ſurrendered to the French on the 5th of February. Some days before the action of the 5th of May, La Romana was charged with the difficult duty of occupying the rear of the enemy by croſſing the frontier of the Pyrenees. French Cerdagne was accordingly invaded, but juſt when the expedition gave promiſe of a ſucceſsful iſſue, the peace of Bâle—to which Manuel Godoi, Duke of Alcudia, was indebted for his title of "*Principe de la Paz*"—was ſigned on the 22nd of July, 1795, by Don Domingo d'Yriarte and M. Barthélemy. Urrutia immediately reſigned his command in Catalonia, and La Romana, now a lieutenant-general, accompanied by his friend, the Count de Lumiares, afterwards known under the name of Prince Pio, retired to Alicante, to devote himſelf to the ſtudy of antiquities.

In

In 1798, the English having taken possession of Minorca, La Romana was appointed to the command of a body of troops who were to be employed in the recapture of that island; but the expedition never sailed, owing to the disaster which befel the Spanish squadron at Trafalgar.

In 1800 La Romana was named commandant-general, *ad interim*, of Catalonia, where he distinguished himself by his vigorous administration, and subsequently he was called to take a seat in the Supreme Council of War.

In January, 1807, Bonaparte induced the Spanish Government to place at his disposal 14,000 of their best troops to form a corps of observation on the frontiers of Hanover, and close the mouths of the Weser and the Elbe against the English. The Prince of the Peace proposed at first to give the command of this contingent to General Castaños or to O'Farill, but at last determined to place it under the orders of La Romana, who was accordingly summoned to Madrid. After a good deal of hesitation, which the very marked dissatisfaction of Strogonoff, the Russian minister at Madrid, tended to increase,* the Prince of the

* Strogonoff suggested a fear that the Spanish troops might be *republicanised* by coming into contact with the French

the Peace—who, in this affair, ſeems to have yielded reluctantly to the wiſhes of Bonaparte —not willing or not daring to reſiſt his reiterated and threatening importunities--at laſt gave the order for departure; and 8,000 or 9,000 Spaniſh auxiliaries commenced their march in the month of May, taking their route through the French territory. They were to be joined by a diviſion of 6,000 Spaniards then quartered in Tuſcany. Theſe arrived at the place of rendezvous before La Romana, and aſſiſted in the ſiege of Stralſund.

La Romana was accuſtomed openly to expreſs his regret that Spain was ſo far behind other European nations in her induſtry and in the adoption of liberal ideas. Well pleaſed, therefore, as he was with the opportunity afforded him of improving his own knowledge of the art of war, while he took part in the military operations of the French, he found equal pleaſure in the anticipation that his troops, being of neceſſity brought into frequent contact with their allies, would acquire notions of liberty which might afterwards

French, and intimated beſides that this ſtep on the part of the Spaniſh government would be regarded by Ruſſia as a hoſtile proceeding; but his cautions and his menaces were alike diſregarded.

afterwards be usefully developed and propagated in Spain.

The Spanish troops having been placed under the supreme command of Bernadotte, acted in concert with the French against Swedish Pomerania, and while so employed made themselves conspicuous by their courage and their discipline. After the peace of Tilsit, in July, 1807, war having then broken out between England and Denmark, and Bonaparte having conceived the design of invading Sweden, the Spanish troops were ordered to the Danish Islands, with a view to their forming the vanguard of Bernadotte's army. They landed in successive divisions during the months of March, April, and May, 1808, in Seeland, Jutland, and Fünen, and were there cantoned.

It was at this time that Bonaparte, by adroitly fomenting the ill-feeling between Charles IV. and his son, and by the alternate use of craft, perfidy, and violence, succeeded in depriving both those princes of the crown, and consigning them and their family to captivity. La Romana was in Fünen, when Bernadotte communicated to him the order of Bonaparte, that he should take an oath of allegiance to Joseph Napoleon, whom he called the new sovereign of Spain, and administer the same oath

oath to his troops. In the delicate position in which the Spanish general was placed, almost surrounded by a French force vastly superior to his own—held in check by the Danish troops also, and shut out from any direct communication with his native country,—he felt himself compelled to yield to the torrent for awhile, that he might not compromise the safety of the large body of men under his command; but the oath, in the terms in which he studiously couched it, was a conditional one, pre-supposing the unanimous consent of the Spanish nation. When, a little while after this, authentic information of the actual state of affairs in Spain was brought to him by an ecclesiastic, who encountered a thousand dangers before he reached him, La Romana at first hesitated to act.* But when Don Vincente Lobo, a Spanish officer, commissioned by the Junta of Seville, and then on board the English fleet in the Baltic, had found means to put him in possession of despatches from the different Juntas, and

* There is some inexactness in this statement. It will be seen by the foregoing narrative, that the information brought to La Romana by Mr. Robertson (the ecclesiastic here mentioned) was sufficient to decide his course of action, and that he announced his resolution in their last interview. Ed.

and a letter from General Morla, containing details regarding the invaſion of the French, the inſurrection of the Spaniards, and the capture of the French fleet ſtationed at Cadiz, he determined to throw off the maſk at once and fly to the defence of his country.

After a few meſſages had paſſed between him and Rear-Admiral Keats, the ſecond in command of the Engliſh fleet, he came to a full underſtanding with that officer as to the meaſures which were to be taken to effect the deliverance of the Spaniſh troops. He pretended, nevertheleſs, to yield to the arguments of Marſhal Bernadotte, who bitterly complained of the conditional form in which he had adminiſtered the oath; he even promiſed to ſubſtitute for that form any other that might be preſcribed to him; but he at the ſame time (Auguſt 6th) addreſſed an energetic circular to the commanding officers of the different corps under his orders, informing them of the events which had taken place in Spain, apprizing them of the courſe of action he had reſolved upon, and inviting them all to aſſemble themſelves immediately in the iſles of Fünen and Langeland, ſo that the French might have no opportunity of obſtructing their noble deſign. "I am a Spaniard," ſaid La Romana in this circular, "and

"and I am resolved to share the glorious destiny of my native land. Anything is preferable to the life of idle dependence that we lead, and I have fully made up my mind to embark with the troops who are willing to follow me." The orders of La Romana were so punctually and so secretly carried into effect, that almost all the Spanish troops, though setting out from different points, arrived nearly on the same day at the place of rendezvous. None failed to make their appearance except the corps stationed in Seeland, who had been disarmed and made prisoners of war in the arsenal at Copenhagen,* and two squadrons that suffered the like hard fortune in Jutland. Three companies of Danes were in garrison at Nyborg, in Fünen. La Romana, fearing lest these should in any way thwart his

* This corps, composed of six battalions of the regiments of the Asturias and Guadalaxara, to the number of nearly 4,000, had been cantoned at or near Röskilde. They had obstinately refused to take the oath of allegiance to Joseph, broken out into open revolt, and even murdered a French adjutant. Ultimately they were pacified and disarmed. Besides being strongly actuated by a sentiment of loyalty to their lawful sovereign, they were deeply offended by a French officer having been empowered to administer the oath to them instead of their own general, La Romana.

his plans, contrived to get them withdrawn by means of a counterfeit order from the Prince of Ponte Corvo; he then, in ſpite of the reſiſtance and remonſtrances of the Daniſh governor, took poſſeſſion himſelf of this important place, where there were gunboats in the harbour which might have annoyed him, but which he made ſubſervient to the execution of his purpoſe. After he had concluded a convention with the Governor of Langeland, by which the latter engaged to ſupply him with whatever quantity of proviſions the iſland could furniſh, the Spaniſh troops, to the number of nearly 10,000 men, were embarked on board ſome Daniſh coaſting-veſſels which were then lying at Nyborg and Langeland, and were joined at Gothenburg by La Romana and his ſtaff, who had been conveyed thither in Engliſh veſſels. La Romana, leaving the command of the troops to the Count de San Romano, went directly to London to make arrangements with the Engliſh miniſtry regarding the ſubſidies which were indiſpenſably requiſite for the vigorous proſecution of the war. He did not land in Spain until after the battle of Eſpinoſa, on 11th of November, 1808, in which Blake was entirely defeated by the united corps of Le Fèvre, Maiſon, and Victor; and the troops which had then recently

recently arrived from Denmark having been disembarked at Santander on the 9th of October, were nearly all cut to pieces.

La Romana, who had been appointed commandant-in-chief of the northern provinces of Spain, did not allow himself to be cast down by this disaster, or by the reverses which the English and Spanish armies had experienced in other quarters; he gathered together the shattered remnants of the army which had been defeated at Espinosa, and endeavoured to awaken fresh energy in the inhabitants of the country over which they had been dispersed.

In a proclamation which he published in January, 1809, he censures the disorder which had characterized the retreat upon Leon, as well as the cowardice of some officers who had abandoned their flag, and complains in general of the relaxation of discipline. Fully persuaded that the late reverses were to be ascribed to the timidity or the inexpertness of the chiefs, he established various punishments for such as should not perform their duty. The Junta of Asturias had evinced great negligence in providing for the defence of the country; he dissolved it by military authority, in virtue of the powers confided to him by the Supreme Junta, and replaced it by a new assembly,

assembly, the members of which were named by himself. He explained his reasons for what he had done in a proclamation dated 2nd of May, 1809.

We will not follow La Romana through the various actions in which he was engaged with the French in Galicia and the Asturias between February and July, 1809. We need only say that his force, after the retreat of the English, being reduced to a feeble corps of 6,000 men, imperfectly disciplined, he was obliged to adopt a different method of carrying on the war; and that, nevertheless, through the influence of the example which he set his soldiers in patiently and courageously supporting fatigues and privations of every kind, he succeeded, by means of rapid and repeated movements, in harassing the armies of Ney and Soult to such a degree, that they found themselves compelled to evacuate that part of Spain over which his command extended. This is a brilliant epoch in his military career.

On the 10th of July, 1809, he published a proclamation at Corunna against the traitors who, seduced by the gold of Bonaparte, were endeavouring to sow dissensions among Spaniards, and to excite distrust against the central Junta. This same Junta, on the other hand, summoned him, on the 31st of

August,

August, to take his ſeat amongſt its members —either wiſhing to profit by his counſels, or, perhaps, intent on removing him from his command.* However this may be, it left him to chooſe his own ſucceſſor. La Romana, who feared nothing ſo much as civil war, obeyed without heſitation, diſregarding the advice of ſome of his friends, who would have perſuaded him to retain his command. In the proclamation by which he informed his troops of his departure and of the new functions he was about to aſſume, he reminded them of the retreat from Portugal and the brilliant actions of Villa Franca, Vigo, Lugo, Santiago and San Payo. He at the ſame time transferred the command of the army to Major-General Don Gabriel de Mendezabal, and the government of Galicia to the Count de Noronha, the vice-commandant and preſident of the Royal Audience.

On the 15th of October, he addreſſed a repreſentation to the Supreme Junta concerning the exiſting form of the government, and the form which ſhould be adopted to bring it into harmony with the conſtitutional principles of the monarchy. In this addreſs he ſhowed

* The ſomewhat arbitrary manner in which La Romana had diſſolved the Junta of the Aſturias had raiſed enemies againſt him.

ſhowed himſelf adverſe to the repreſentative ſyſtem on which the exiſtence of the Junta itſelf was baſed, but which he conſidered as ſavouring of democracy rather than monarchy. Then, reviewing the promiſes of the Junta, which among other things had announced that it would organize an army of 500,000 infantry and 50,000 cavalry, he compares theſe promiſes with the reſults. "The nation complains," ſaid he, "of the inſufficiency of the force deſtined for its defence, and that inſtead of ſalutary reforms, new abuſes have been introduced." He charged the Junta further with having exceeded its powers, and with having confided the adminiſtration of affairs to perſons either incompetent or of doubtful loyalty. He propoſed that until the Cortes ſhould be aſſembled, the ſupreme authority ſhould be entruſted to a regent, or to a council of regency compoſed of from three to five perſons.

The advice of La Romana was not liſtened to. After the defeat of the Spaniards at Ocaña, on the 18th of November, 1809, the Supreme Junta directed that he, with Don Rodrigo Riquelme, ſhould repair to the head-quarters at Carolina, armed with the moſt ample authority to take meaſures, in concert with Don Juan Dios Galienez Roba, the commiſſary

miſſary for the army of La Mancha, for the prevention of ſimilar calamities in future. La Romana refuſed to accept a commiſſion which he deemed uſeleſs, or, at any rate, beneath him in dignity.

In 1810 he was again employed in active ſervice, being appointed to the command of the army of the left. Re-entering Caſtile in the month of Auguſt, with 25,000 men, he was reinforced on the 28th of November, at Alba de Tormes, by the remains of the diviſion of Balleſteros, five days after the check which that diviſion met with on the banks of the river from which the town juſt mentioned takes its name. When the news reached him of the movements of the French troops in Eſtremadura, of the difficulty encountered in ſuccouring Olivença, and of the poſſibility that Badajoz might be attacked, he marched his troops rapidly into that province. He was indulging hopes of being able to drive the French beyond its frontier, when he received an urgent ſummons from Lord Wellington to haſten to the aſſiſtance of the allied troops, who were menaced by the forces under the command of Maſſena. La Romana arrived in Portugal in the beginning of January, 1811, but on the 23rd of the ſame month he died in the city of Cartaxo, after a ſhort illneſs. His body,

body, after having been embalmed, was conveyed to Lisbon in an English vessel, and his entrails, enclosed in a richly ornamented chest, were buried with extraordinary pomp in the monastery of Belem. "His virtues, his talents, and his patriotism were well known to the Government of his Britannic Majesty," said Lord Wellington, in a despatch which he addressed on the 26th of January, 1811, to the Earl of Liverpool. "In him the Spanish army has lost its greatest ornament, his country her purest patriot, and the world the bravest and most zealous defender of the cause for which we are in arms. I shall always acknowledge with gratitude the assistance I have received from him in the field, as well as in council, since he joined this army."

His withdrawal from Denmark, and his campaign in Galicia and the Asturias, will secure to La Romana an honourable place among the Spanish commanders who have deserved well of their country. His personal bravery was of the highest stamp, but the composure which he displayed under fire was a quality which did not invariably contribute to his success as a general. In its outward aspect his character wanted force; he was averse to reflection, and disposed to adopt the conflicting opinions of those who surrounded him,

him, each in its turn. This changefulneſs was by no means to be attributed to a want of conviction; it was in perfect good-faith that he often declared himſelf directly oppoſed to an opinion which he had recently embraced with ardour. He was generous and bountiful, eſpecially towards thoſe who had endeavoured to injure him; affable with all, but moſt of all with his ſoldiers, by whom he was adored. But theſe good qualities were obſcured, in ſome degree, by his eccentricities, which were ſometimes of a kind to injure his reputation. Though converſant with literature, and delighting in it, La Romana was not to be claſſed with men of learning, but he had a highly cultivated mind, and was endowed with a prodigious memory. He had a familiar knowledge of Greek, Latin, and four living languages. He could diſcuſs with equal facility a queſtion in medicine or a point of law, a mathematical problem or a fact in hiſtory. The moſt preſſing dangers never diſturbed his daily practice of reading ſome of the odes of Pindar, or ſome paſſages from Xenophon and others of the Greek authors, to whom he was devotedly attached. Natural ſcience had great attractions for him, and he poſſeſſed a cabinet filled with all kinds of inſtruments connected with it. He had another

cabinet

cabinet of mineralogy, and a third which contained ſome fine paintings of the Valentian ſchool. He was a painter himſelf, it is ſaid, and not an unſucceſsful one; he made very agreeable verſes, and he is known to have rendered highly important aid to the Count of Lumiares in his reſearches into antiquity.

Extract from Bourienne's Memoirs of Napoleon.

Previous to the interview at Erfurt, an event took place which created a ſtrong intereſt in Hamburg, and throughout Europe; an event which was planned and executed with inconceivable ſecreſy. I allude to the defection of the Marquis de la Romana, which I have not hitherto noticed, in order that I might not ſeparate the different facts which came to my knowledge relative to that defection, and the circumſtances which accompanied it.

The Marquis de la Romana had come to the Hanſe Towns at the head of a corps of 18,000 men, which the Emperor, in the preceding campaign, claimed in virtue of treaties previouſly concluded with the Spaniſh Government. The Spaniſh troops at firſt

met

met with a good reception in the Hanſe Towns. The difference of language, indeed, occaſionally cauſed diſcord; but when better acquainted, the inhabitants and their viſitors became good friends. The Marquis de la Romana was a little ſwarthy man, of unprepoſſeſſing, and rather common, appearance; but he had a conſiderable ſhare of talent and information. He had travelled in almoſt every part of Europe; and as he had been a cloſe obſerver of all he ſaw, his converſation was exceedingly agreeable and inſtructive. During his ſtay at Hamburg, General Romana ſpent almoſt every evening at my houſe, and invariably fell aſleep over a game at whiſt. Madame de Bourienne was uſually his partner, and I recollect he perpetually offered apologies for his involuntary breach of good manners. This, however, did not hinder him from being guilty of the ſame offence the next evening. I will preſently explain the cauſe of this regular ſieſta.

On the King of Spain's birthday, the Marquis de la Romana gave a magnificent entertainment. The decorations of the ball-room conſiſted of military attributes. The Marquis did the honors with infinite grace, and paid particular attention to the French Generals. He always ſpoke of the Emperor in very reſpectful

ſpectful terms, without any appearance of affectation, ſo that it was impoſſible to ſuſpect him of harbouring any bad deſign. He played his part to the laſt with the utmoſt addreſs.

At Hamburg we had already received intelligence of the fatal reſult of the battle of the Sierra Morena, and of the capitulation of Dupont, which diſgraced him at the very moment when the whole army marked him out as the man moſt likely to receive the bâton of Marſhal of France.

Meanwhile, the Marquis de la Romana departed for the Daniſh Iſland of Fünen, in compliance with the order which General Bernadotte had tranſmitted to him. There, as at Hamburg, the Spaniards were well liked, for their General obliged them to obſerve the ſtricteſt diſcipline. Great preparations were made at Hamburg on the approach of St. Napoleon's day, which was then celebrated with much ſolemnity in every town in which France had repreſentatives. The Prince of Ponte Corvo was then at Travemunde, a ſmall ſeaport near Lübeck; but that did not prevent him from giving directions for the feſtival of the 15th of Auguſt. The Marquis de la Romana, the better to deceive the Marſhal, diſpatched a courier, requeſting permiſſion to viſit Hamburg on the day of the fête, in order

to

to join his prayers to thoſe of the French, and to receive on the day of the fête, from the hands of the Prince, the Grand Order of the Legion of Honor, which he had ſolicited, and which Napoleon had granted him. Three days after, Bernadotte received intelligence of the defection of La Romana.

The Marquis aſſembled a great number of Engliſh veſſels on the coaſt, and eſcaped with all his troops, except a depôt of 600 men left at Altona.

We afterwards heard that he experienced no interruption in his paſſage, and that he landed with his troops at Corunna.

I now knew to what to attribute the drowſineſs which always overcame the Marquis de la Romana when he ſat down to take a hand at whiſt. The fact was, he ſat up all night making preparations for the eſcape which he had long meditated, while to lull ſuſpicion he ſhowed himſelf everywhere during the day, as uſual.

On the defection of the Spaniſh troops, I received letters from Government, requiring me to augment my vigilance, and to ſeek out thoſe perſons who might have been in the confidence of the Marquis de la Romana. I was informed that Engliſh agents diſperſed through the Hanſe Towns were endeavouring to foment diſcord.

The

The following extract from Bourienne relates to the period immediately preceding the defection of Romana, and shows the stratagems resorted to by Bonaparte to keep the Spaniards in complete ignorance of the state of affairs in Spain.

"On the 6th April following, I received a second letter from Bernadotte, in which he desired me to order the Grand Ducal post-master to keep back all letters addressed to the Spanish troops who had been placed under his command, and of which the corps of Romana formed a part.

"The post-master was directed to keep the letters until he received orders to forward them to their destination. Bernadotte considered this step indispensable to prevent the intrigues which he feared might be set on foot in order to shake the fidelity of the Spaniards he commanded."

Extract

Extract from Napier's Peninsular War.

WITH Mr. Frere came a fleet conveying a Spanish force under the Marquis of Romana. When the insurrection first broke forth, that nobleman commanded fourteen or fifteen thousand troops serving with the French armies. Castaños, through Sir Hugh Dalrymple, desired the British Government to apprise Romana that Spain was in arms, and extricate his army, and Mr. McKenzie was selected by the Ministers to conduct the enterprise. The Spaniards were in Holstein, Sleswig, Jutland, and the islands of Fünen, Zealand, and Langeland. McKenzie, through the medium of one Robertson, a Catholic priest, opened a communication with Romana, and neither the General nor soldiers hesitated. Sir Richard Keats then appeared off Nyborg in the island of Fünen, with a squadron detached from the Baltic fleet, a majority of the Spanish regiments, quartered in Sleswig immediately seized all the craft in the harbours, and pushed across the channel to Fünen, where Romana, with the assistance of Keats, had seized the port and castle of Nyborg, without opposition save from a small Danish

Danish ship of war moored in the harbour. From thence the Spaniards passed to Langeland, where they embarked nine thousand strong on board the English fleet commanded by Sir James Saumarez. The rest of the troops either remained in Sleswig, or were disarmed by the Danish forces in Zealand. This enterprise was ably conducted, and the readiness of the Spanish soldiery was very honourable, yet the danger was slight to all save Mr. Robertson. Romana, after visiting England, repaired to Corunna, but his troops landed at St. Andrew, where they were equipped from the English stores, and then proceeded by divisions to join Blake's army in Biscay.

Note.—Our narrative explains that Mr. McKenzie's part was, from the beginning, merely secondary or intermediate, he having been directed to accompany Mr. R. to Heligoland, and there to remain to receive and forward any communications which Mr. R. might send to him.—*Ed.*

CHISWICK PRESS:—PRINTED BY WHITTINGHAM AND WILKINS, TOOKS COURT, CHANCERY LANE.